BREAKING THE SKIN
21ST CENTURY IRISH WRITING

Published: 18th October 2002
by The Black Mountain Press
P O Box 9, Ballyclare, County Antrim, BT39 0JW, N Ireland
www.blackmountainpress.com

Poem Copyrights © the Authors, 2002
Introduction Copyrights © Nigel McLoughlin, Matthew Fluharty and Frank Sewell

The Black Mountain Press gratefully acknowledges the financial assistance of The Arts Council of Northern Ireland and the National Lottery Fund

ISBN: 0-9537570-2-1

The moral right of the authors has been asserted. A catalogue record for this book is available from the British Library. All rights reserved. No part of this publication may be transmitted in any form or by any means, electronic or mechanical, including photography, recording or any information storage or retrieval system, without permission in writing from the publisher. The book is sold subject to the condition that it shall not, by way of trade or otherwise, be lent, resold or otherwise circulated without the publisher's prior consent in any form of binding or cover other than that in which it is published and without a similar condition, including this condition, being imposed on the subsequent publisher.

Cover design by Miriam de Búrca
Typesetting by Tonic Design, Belfast
Printed by Easyprint, Belfast

BREAKING THE SKIN
21ST CENTURY IRISH WRITING

VOLUME TWO: NEW POETRY

Edited by
Nigel McLoughlin & Matthew Fluharty

Irish Section edited by Frankie Sewell

ACKNOWLEDGEMENTS

Acknowledgement is made to Nigel McLoughlin, who suggested the title. John Brown, formerly of the Arts Council of Northern Ireland, is thanked for being instrumental in the publication's fruition.

The editors would like to thank all the poets for their newer work and the publishers for their kind permission to use poems from the following volumes:

Airborne, Mark Granier, Salmon Poetry, 2000.
Pictures From A Reservation, Ger Reidy, Dedalus Press, 1998.
Languages, Gary Allen, Flambard/Black Mountain Presses, 2002.
When The Lights Go Up, Cherry Smyth, Lagan Press, 2001.
The Erratic Behaviour Of Tides, Katherine Duffy, Dedalus Press, 1999.
Downpatrick Races, Damian Smyth, Lagan Press, 2000.
A Dog Called Chance, Paula Cunningham, Smith Doorstop, 1999.
Black Wolf On A White Plain, Mary Montague, Summer Palace Press, 2001.
The Blind Woman In The Blue House, Kate Newmann, Summer Palace Press, 2001.
Invitation To The Air, Yvonne Cullen, iTaLiC's Press, 1998
The White Battlefield Of Silence, James McCabe, Dedalus Press, 1999.
Godsong & A Matter Of Honour, Niall McGrath, Black Mountain Press, 2000.
Sailing To Hokkaido, Joseph Woods, Worple Press, 2001.
At The Waters' Clearing, Nigel McLoughlin, Flambard/Black Mountain, 2001.
The Heel Of Bernadette, Colette Bryce, Picador, Macmillan UK, 2000.
The Nowhere Birds, Caitríona O'Reilly, Bloodaxe Books, 2001.
Tulle, Mary O'Donoghue, Salmon Poetry, 2000.
Faoi Chebáiotí Is Ríonacha, Celia de Fréine, Indreabhán, Cló Iar-Chonnachta, 2001
Sruth Teangacha/Stream of Tongues, Gearóid Mac Lochlainn, Indreabhán,
Cló Iar-Chonnachta, 2002
An Chéad Chló, Tarlach MacGongáil, ed. Cathal Ó Searcaigh, Indreabhán,
Cló Iar-Chonnachta, 1997
Idir Dhá Ghleann, Colette Ní Ghallchóir, Dublin, Coiscéim, 1999

And to the following poets for work included in collections which are to be published in the next two years: John O Donnell, Adrian Fox, Michael Begnal, Deirdre Cartmill, Kevin Higgins & Nell Regan.

The poets and the editors also extend their thanks to the editors of the various literary journals which first published some of the poems reproduced here, without these outlets poetry would surely founder on the rock of indifference.

Other volumes by poets included here, which are in print are:

Bar Talk, Nessa O'Mahony, iTaLiC's Press, 1999.
Day Release, Aidan Rooney-Céspedes, Gallery Press, 2000.
Touching The Bones, Tom French, Gallery Press, 2001.

PREFACE

In prefacing this anthology, I am conscious of two things, firstly that I am writing about people who are at the same sensitive stage in their poetic careers as myself and secondly that there are some who, through just having published their second collection or by not having a collection formally accepted at the time of writing, lie outside the criteria for this anthology. As regards the first instance, I will keep my observations general and as regards the second, the observations are no less applicable to those poets as they are to those who fell within the remit.

It may be noticed from those appearing here that this 'generation' of poets, if I may loosely call them that, have on average published later than their predecessors. The youngest here is twenty-seven, once the average age for a first collection. This long apprenticeship to their craft is, I think, one of three things that mark this 'generation' out. Another is the fact that here we perhaps are seeing the first flush of 'superhighway poets' who cast their poems adrift on the vast sea of the internet to end up in journals in Canada, Australia, Japan, Europe, New Zealand and God knows where else. They are perhaps more widely published than previous generations were at the same stage of development.

The last, is the fact that influence has been absorbed to the same degree inwards, these are a diasporic generation who have, or currently do, live in Asia, Europe, Africa, Australia and America. They bring with them rich and unusual images from the ends of the earth, internalise them and attempt relation to, and study of, their sense of Irishness. They use Irish, French, Italian etc with impunity if the English fails them and another language says it better. They are intrinsically demanding, formally free, taking their inspiration where they find it without apology.

Yeats' admonition to 'sing whatever is well made' has also been heeded. Here is a generation who are musically adept, but who have studied their craft long and hard enough to be capable of burying the music deep into the grain of the poem, until it is background or alternatively can push it front and centre in a symphony of sounds. The variety of style, tone, image, form and experiment is wide and well matured.

The old ideological division between the North and the South has all but disappeared, here are poets who are as conscious of style and content, who can both 'think and sing'. These are poets of the world and world poets, but all are unmistakeably Irish – the tradition burns through their work no less brightly for being added to by American, English and European traditions and influences. Jimmy Simmons used to tell his MA students to 'stop scratching at the surface' – here are new young poets who have all broken the skin.

Nigel McLoughlin.

Nigel McLoughlin
Born in 1968 in Enniskillen, he now lives and works in Falcarragh. He holds an MA in Creative Writing from Lancaster University and is currently working towards his PhD with the same university. He previously has been guest Poetry Editor for The New Writer and has taught Poetics and Form at Poets' House. Most recently he has just finished a stint as Writer-In-Residence in Fermanagh, working with groups from Fermanagh, Cavan and Leitrim.

Matthew Fluharty
Born in 1976 in Ohio, he now lives and works in Boston. He holds an MA in Creative Writing from Lancaster University having previously graduated Beloit College with degrees in Creative Writing, Literary Studies and Journalism. He was recently Poet-In-Residence at New Light Studios, Wisconsin and previously Poetry Advisor to The Missouri Review and special intern at The Beloit Fiction Journal. His work has been published in America, Ireland and the UK. His first collection is forthcoming.

INTRODUCTION

In the spring of 2000, Nigel McLoughlin and I spent our evenings gathered around the classroom table at Poet's House, talking poetry and sharing bottles of wine and whiskey. That season we were finishing our studies and progressing towards a cohesive body of work, that enigmatic first collection. To get there, we needed to figure for ourselves questions of style and content, and how to move from the waves of influence toward an authentic voice.

In the midst of this, one night when the bottle got low, the concept for this book came into being. We started a list of poets whose body of work addressed the issues we were raising in our late night roundtable. It became a sort of quest, paging through recent magazines and journals, exchanging trans-Atlantic telephone calls. As the idea progressed we welcomed Frankie Sewell into the fold to edit the Irish language section of a book that appeared to just want to grow and grow. It would, after all, have been incomplete without the presence of those emerging poets in Ireland's mother tongue. When John McAllister came aboard to edit the prose volume, we realised we had something that was going to be really exciting.

The decision to have an Irish section as opposed to allowing the poets to appear scattered through the book, was taken for two reasons, firstly that we wanted to allow these poets also to interact on a generational level and secondly because different criteria were applied to the choice of poets in the Irish language. After these months, and with the good graces of Black Mountain Press, we present *Breaking The Skin: an anthology of young emerging Irish poets.*

The idea of focusing an anthology around the work of emerging young Irish poets is a daunting and dodgy task. What makes a poet young, emerging, or Irish, for that matter? Out of a wide field of definitions, we offer this – a selection of poets Irish by birth or citizenship under 45 who have published one book or have one collection forthcoming.

This standard excludes a number of poets working towards a first collection, as well as those with two books to their credit, not to mention a handful of fine poets who have moved to Ireland and into the uncertain realm of diaspora. There also were a few poets who, for various reasons, were unable to submit. It is our hope that future editors and publishers will expand our efforts into collections that include these others, to add to the company within these pages.

These poets are enjoying high visibility thanks to a solid contingent of fine magazines that are unhesitant to publish emerging voices. *Cyphers, Fortnight, Metre, Poetry Ireland, HU, Burning Bush* and others, as well as newer journals such as *The SHOp, West 47* and *Black Mountain Review*, are welcoming these new faces to share space with the established order of Irish poetry. As a result, we are treated to a dramatic recalibration of existing themes and are led into fresh fields.

The intense world-historical conscience of James McCabe and Kate Newmann compliment the many re-evaluations of what it means to be Irish in the next millennium. Michael Begnal's disembodied voice, Tom French's "Estate," or Aiden Rooney-Céspedes' "The Name Takers" mine that ambiguity between cliché and cultural heritage.

Likewise, this group of poets offer a new perspective on the conflict in 'The North'. Colette Bryce, Deirdre Cartmill and Cherry Smyth witnessed the events as children and young women. When read with Gary Allen and John O'Donnell we have a remarkable document of an entire generation coming to terms with a social identity independent from political dogma.

Damien Smyth's "Imagine Belfast" lists in length and ambition with McLoughlin's "Lines" and Joe Woods' "Sicilian Sketches," sound companions to the epigrammatic odes of Mark Granier and the conceptual inventiveness of Adrian Fox's "Half a Sestina for Stephanie" and Nessa O'Mahony's "Venice Postcards." The English language section reaches an appropriate close in the distilled imagery of Mary O'Donoghue and Caitríona O'Reilly.

But, in the end, all of these poets resist critical handles. The old divisions between north and south, rural and urban, lyric and narrative still exist, but this group seems unwilling to conform to the rigidity of these schools. Whether this is a product of the internet age or an effect of growing up under the radar of postmodernism remains to be seen. Regardless, these poets exert a tremendous range and possess remarkable abilities. Enough so that poetry students will still gather around tables, trying to figure out what's going to happen next.

Matthew Fluharty

CONTENTS

Mark Granier *b. 1957*
Fall Note 16
Axe Heads In The Natural History Museum 17
Driving Through The Sally Gap 18
Drawing Room 19
Fractal Highways 20
Lines For The Diceman 21

Ger Reidy *b. 1958*
The Gap is Closing 22
Slievemore Deserted Village 23
November Day 24
Winter Evening 26
Beloved 27
Marooned 28
Lame Dogs 29

Gary Allen *b. 1959*
First Love 31
Linen 32
Sisyphus 33
Fire-Watcher 34
The Workhouse 35
Early Morning, North Antrim 36
The Brick Factory 37

John O'Donnell *b. 1960*
The Shipping Forecast 38
Christmas 1914 39
Missing Persons 41
The Match 42

This Afternoon	44
What The Tide Brings In	45

Adrian Fox *b. 1961*

New York 2001: Fragment	46
Half A Sestina For Stephanie	48
Radio Realism	49
The Light On The Stones	50
A Tricolour In Tatters	51
Blue	52

Cherry Smyth *b. 1961*

Human Image	53
In Residence	54
In The South That Winter	55
The End Of July	56
The Roadside	58
Water	60

Katherine Duffy *b. 1962*

Season	61
Bilingual	62
Planet DIY	63
Transaction	64
Fuchsia City	65
Bubblewrapped	66
Restorers V. The Ceiling Vandal	67

Damian Smyth *b. 1962*

The Mighty Arkle	68
Inside	69
Imagine Belfast	70

Paula Cunningham *b. 1963*

Losing The Keys	77

Collage 78
Sometimes Dancing 79
Aubade 80
Mother's Pride 81
Seeing Things 82

Mary Montague b. 1964
The Shepherdess 84
December's Close 86
Afterwards 87
First Day In Cape Breton 89

Nessa O'Mahony b. 1964
Fin de Siecle 91
I Ching 92
Valentia Sunset 93
Hit Delete 94
They're Grand When You Can Give Them Back 95
Venice Postcards 96

Kate Newmann b. 1965
Gabriela Mistral, Nobel Prize Winner 98
Pablo Neruda's House In Valparaiso 99
Pushkin's Honeymoon House 100
Swan Lake At The Mariinsky Theatre 101
The Roof Tiles 102
What The Spanish Brought 103
White Crosses 104

Aidan Rooney-Céspedes b. 1965
Lynx 105
Francis Bacon And The Hen 106
The Visit 107
The Name Takers 108
Survival 110
Why Muldoon 112

Michael S. Begnal *b. 1966*
Expatriation 113
Ancestor Worship 114
New Year's Day 1999 116
View From A Galway Window 118
Seal Poem 119

Yvonne Cullen *b. 1966*
From: Invitation To The Air 120

Tom French *b. 1966*
Estate 128
Two Verbs For 'To Be' 129
Blood 130
Listening Test 131
Saint Anthony Preaches To The Fish 132
Nationalism In Music 133

James McCabe *b. 1966*
Eagle's Nest 134
Clare Island Revisited 135
An Angel Surveys The Ruins Of Dresden 136
Soundings 137
Oradour Sur Glane 138

Niall McGrath *b. 1966*
Moon Calf 142
Aurora Borealis 143
In The Piggery 144
From Njal's Saga, Section 157 145

Joseph Woods *b. 1966*
Sicilian Sketches 149
Mrs Moon 155
Cagayan de Oro 156

Deirdre Cartmill *b. 1967*
Night Watch 158
Aftermath 159
Drive By 160
Long Home 161
Monolithic Venus 163
Karaoke In The Glasshouse 165

Kevin Higgins *b. 1967*
A Brief History Of Those Who Made Their
Point Politely And Then Went Home 167
By Five O'Clock 168
January 169
Estrangement: A Sequence 170
Knives 171
Letter To A Friend About Girls 172
To Hell And Back again 173
To Certain Lyric Poets 174

Nigel McLoughlin *b. 1968*
Forty Shades Of Fuchsia 175
High Water 176
Butterfly's Bones 178
Song For No Voices 179
Baile An Easa 180
Lines 181

Nell Regan *b. 1969*
Aspects Of Prometheus (i) 184
A Sense Of Place 185
Ginestra 188
After The Funeral 189
Light 190

Colette Bryce *b.1970*
Footings 191

Break	192
Stones	193
Young	194
Owl	195
Form	196
The Word	198

Caitríona O'Reilly b. 1973

On A Dropped Feather	200
Two Night Time Pieces	201
Blueness	203
The Harbour In January	204
Autobiography	205

Mary O'Donoghue b. 1975

The Textures	207
Jezebel's Palms	208
The She-Machines	210
Lavoisin And Lavigoreux	212
Bova	213

Celia de Fréine

Mochthráth an Mhic Tíre/ *The hour of the wolf*	217
Comhthionól/ *Lobby*	220
Ag tástáil, ag tástáil/ *Testing, testing...*	222
A leannáin/ *Lover*	224
A Dheirfiúracha Dílse/ *Dear sisters*	226
Lámhachta?/ *Taken out and shot?*	228

Gearóid MacLochlainn b. 1967

Daoine nach luaitear/ *Unsung Heroes*	231
Aistriúcháin/ *Translations*	233
Rogha an fhile/ *The poet's choice*	236
Brionglóid Dheireanach Chrazyhorse/ *Crazyhorse's last dream*	239

Colette Ní Ghallchóir
Dealán an Aoibhnis/*Sparkler*   245
Billy Wright/*Billy Wright*   246
Buíochas/*Thanks a lot*   247
Éalú/*Escape*   248
I nGairdín na n-Úll/*In the Orchard*   250

Tarlach MacCongáil b. 1976
An tUaireadóir/*The Watch*   252
Crá an Scoláire/*The Scholar*   254

Mary Reid b. 1953
Brocach/*Badgers' den*   255

MARK GRANIER

BORN IN LONDON IN 1957 AND RAISED IN DUBLIN. HIS POEMS HAVE APPEARED IN NUMEROUS JOURNALS AND NEWSPAPERS IN IRELAND AND THE UK, INCLUDING THE IRISH TIMES, POETRY IRELAND REVIEW, THE SPECTATOR AND THE TLS, AND ON THE IRISH WRITERS' CENTRE WEBSITE ANTHOLOGY:WWW.WRITERSCENTRE.IE/ANTHOLOGY/GRANIER.HTML. HE HAS ALSO READ MANY POEMS BY HIMSELF AND OTHERS ON LYRIC FM. HIS COLLECTION, 'AIRBORNE', WAS PUBLISHED BY SALMON PUBLISHING IN 2000.

Fall Note

The blurred, flamy tide
has laid its long acre
under the hedges, on pavements.

All the colours of earth
have come down to earth to give
thresh-music to walking.

We get the drift: *Let the ground*
be papered in write-offs. Warm
to this covering. I sweep the twelve steps

from our front door to the street,
each bristly, fine-tuning *shhh!*
clearing the shelves,

setting the lines straight.
Now, if I can take that sound
into my head...

Axe Heads In The National History Museum

Behind the warm glass they are in flight,
each one throwing its weight,

polished stone, bronze: tail-wings
migrating in new formations

more and more slow
between the swing and the blow.

Driving Through The Sally Gap

Above Glencree,
the car bounces and the road rises
on wind-cured air, swatches of silky gloom.

The TV mast over on Kippure
is the only whisker of anything
four-walled or closed-in.

Cloud-browsed, darkening shoulders
go on down into a nesting ground
for the ghosts of glaciers.

Crossroads. A signpost
where a great elk stood, antlers
branching out of the mist,

belling the names: Blessington,
Roundwood, Enniskerry... it's late.
Time for the long way home

where the line bellies and dips,
something with the wind up
galloping away with itself.

Drawing Room

"Afternoon tea", The words are my grandmother's words,
like "drawing room", with its gaze fixed on the garden

where curtains will close when day draws to a close,
its courteous features darkening into the leaves.

What is it has set her, rocking her chair by the window,
squinting at *The Collins Gem Book Of Quotations*,

or her diary of birthdays, drawing together the whole
helplessly widening warp and weft of the family?

Something, something – a life that has gone through her –
finds her there rocking and smiling, closing the pattern

to calmness, afternoon light on the little pages
and her measuring gaze still settling, almost level.

Fractal Highways

Evolution's rush hour
and up they come
from the Underground
to the top of the tower,

amoebas and zebras
viruses and humpbacked whales
termites tapeworms eagles

and brief creatures with briefcases
homing up high-rises,
mountains, motorways

scrambling out of the fierce
escalating spiral staircase
of DNA

into space.

Lines For The Diceman
i.m. Tom McGinty

Good to know you might turn up
in the frieze of faces on Grafton Street,
familiar stranger surprising us
in something from your wardrobe-gallery,

a walking painting say, holding its own
gilded ornate frame, the face
a white mask, Mona Lisa
in a black cat-suit, cracking a murky smile.

Dead-slow, solemnly careful
among eddies of Christmas shoppers, summer dawdlers,
tourists, street-traders, Guards...
mindful of each sound-proofed step, sure-

footed as an acrobat, spaced in, treading your own
high wire. When we looked
at you looking through us
we took in the joke that jumped – a spark of silence –

eye to eye, mind to mind,
across Grafton Street's canyon of swirling clockwork noise.
You're gone now forever (back
into the box with Jack)

and scanning the quickslow, giddy, sedate
everyday street-portrait – its procession
of invisible masks – the eye misses you.
Old Master, Diceman, conductor

of the ungrooved thought, catcher
of the thrown glance, are you still there?

GER REIDY

BORN IN 1958, HE HAS WON NUMEROUS NATIONAL POETRY COMPETITIONS INCLUDING THE ALLINGHAM PRIZE, BOYLE ARTS FESTIVAL POETRY COMPETITION, THE GEORGE MOORE POETRY COMPETITION, THE SOUTH TIPPERARY POETRY COMPETITION AND THE LAOIS WRITER'S WEEKEND POETRY COMPETITION. HIS FIRST COLLECTION, 'PICTURES FROM A RESERVATION', PUBLISHED BY DEDALUS, WAS LAUNCHED AT SLIGO'S SCRÍOBH LITERARY FESTIVAL IN 1998.

The Gap Is Closing

He cuts gorse bushes with a bow saw.
He brings his lunch,
the milk bottle corked with paper.
He plods home across the fields at dark
along by the silent river
and latches the timber gate.

He's bursting with boyish happiness; I surprise him.
"It's going to freeze hard tonight,
I know by the sound of the train", he says.
After milking the Friesian he scolds her manners.
As he drinks his cup of tea and eats his bread
I know his work is his religion.

We couldn't agree on the colour of a blue sky.
But in recent years I find myself
changing into his gear before the railway bridge,
driving long straight roads in third
and at the junction wiping fog
off my side window
in exactly his ominous shape.

Slievemore Deserted Village

Curlew calls over the lake
as the rain clears.
Brittle wisps hiss, like
phone wires to an island.
Low cloud communicates
with famine ridges.

And in the ruins, I imagine
thin limbs of victims
outstretched to bridge the time.
In shame I retreat alone.
Their grandchildren ageing gracefully now
in Pennsylvania and Chicago.

Diminished grass is slowly consumed.
Rushes enjoy a sinister revenge,
their creeping paralysis ruthless
even in the most sacred places.
In the distance a figure approaches,
stumbles across the bog onto a track.

He disappears now and then in the hollows.
Smoked like a Moroccan street trader
he offers me a load of breast turf,
as if boatloads of grain wouldn't leave the quay,
as if magpies wouldn't pick our eyes out,
as if grass wouldn't melt in our mouths.

November Day

On mornings like these
we disturbed the red whiteheads
content as the hares played
and crows perched on their backs.

We marched them to the gate
through a pocket of dawn fog.
The neighbour's cattle, curious,
followed them to a field corner.

They leaped and raced down the road,
sentries posted at all the gaps.
A pigeon fluttered in the hedge
and they were scared into the bog.

Bikes abandoned in the briars
we leaped over the ditch
and galloped up the hill
as the early train from Westport trundled by.

At the crossroads we'd meet McHale
leading a dry cow with a halter.
His black suit shiny with time,
laden with his mother's instructions.

Our space is outside Mrs Murphy's house.
Her window sill collected dung pyramids.
Under the clock we saw geese peers
sideways through holes in canvas bags.

One day we met coming from the fair
Gillespie, riding the mare with the cart empty behind,
and McHale sleeping in the Volkswagen
with the calf sucking his ear.

Suspended on a bar stool in McGing's
I saw a pale winter sunshine discover
cornflakes and bags of oats,
as an old woman chewed tobacco under the stairs.

Among the dark angular figures
my father is paid a few notes
peeled from a wad of twenties
with Davitt's ghost smiling everywhere.

Winter Evening

All I know is that it was a long time ago:
mother in the garden, clothes drying on a bush,
pulling grass from around the roses,
hands sprawled in a valium haze,
my father home early from work, then silence.
As the frost descended, the sound of a showband
in the Temperance Hall came across the bog:
"Take me back to where the grass grows the greenest".
Then time to feed silage to the shorthorns
in the limekiln field, study the Punic wars
and tie a shivering dog to a railway sleeper.
My father watched Hawaii Five-O,
mother wove a basket for charity.
The moon came up over the graveyard,
gleamed through their bedroom window,
and I watch as it caressed them both,
as it absolved the living and the dead.

Beloved

For years I sat in a dry rock pool
drunk with the gravedigger.
One day he was looking for a new engine
for his tractor – a Ferguson 35X.
"I'll have to go across the border,
you can't get the four cylinder model here," he said.
"Will you bring a portable TV across for me?" I asked.
I was stranded, building a stone wall
at the Community Centre on the Back-To-Work Scheme,
and had lost hope of the tide coming in.

We were watching *Sky News* in the Hollywood Bar –
rain spreading from Japan to the Korean peninsula.
I saw his face deformed with terror
as he gazed out to sea.
The light dimmed, a wave splashed over us,
lapping into all my arid cracks.
His bony hands lost their grip.
I can still see him running for the shoreline
anxious to grab his spade.
He looked back aghast.
I never saw him again.
Your shadow descended, my watch stopped.
The last thing I noticed
was your small finger beckon the ocean.

Marooned

Today was borrowed or left over from youth,
the tide gone out, the sea in the distance,
when we adored girls, drank wine and fell asleep.
We would be at the centre of it all soon enough.

Soon I awoke to the deafening ocean.
I was alone, waves surrounded me.
My friends huddled on their own sandbars.
The water too deep now, memories lap at my feet.

Far off my son sleeps unaware on a grassy mound.
Beside me my father's bones are polishing the rocks.

Lame Dogs

Joe who sold a dry cow at the mart
and whose wife died last year
leers at Mary from the barstool,
tells her that she was his first choice.
She laughs with a long wheeze
like a hearse with a puncture,
her pink knickers peek above her knee.
Welcome to the world of support stockings
and discarded bingo sheets in community halls,
old phone bills pressed between faded china cups
and photographs of forgotten relatives
in USA Assorted biscuit tins.
After three gins silence screams the truth
but he is rescued by the 3.30 from Doncaster.
Gillespie - a sub on the minor football team
who won the Connaught Final thirty years ago -
has measured every woman here
but keeps his options open.
Afternoon now, and the race is over,
and killing time a habit too ingrained to stop.
Pretension hangs from him like the lining from a torn coat
and he must wander home in the cruel sunlight
past the drunk pissing on a park bench
and the bank manager's wife teasing a rose bush,
through the gangs of mocking convent girls
and the Pakistani street traders,
gazing at the gleaming cabbage plants
and cheap Knock virgins swinging in the gale.
He stumbles upstairs with a baby Power
to a room overlooking a narrow garden
and the disused railway track beyond,
then falls onto the bed and watches
the billboard shadow creep across the room,

is woken by the sound of the AA traffic report
and the news that Tony Cascarino has pulled a hamstring (again).
He stares vacantly out the back window
at the Up Mayo slogan on the handball alley,
at the girl next door sprawled on the lawn
and the boy in the other garden watching her.
A News of the World pinup looks down on him
but he decides instead to turn on the kettle
and peer into the anaemic fridge.
He'll watch the farming programme on TV
although he's long since sold his rushy fields,
and the silly English quiz show
featuring Larry and the two busty girls.
Then he'll wander into the Shamrock Bar
where the Ibiza crowd are singing karaoke.
Going home he peers at the racing results
in the shop beside the take-away,
stumbles down the centre of a moonlit road.
The heart sinks with familiar sadness,
sharing this appalling beauty with himself.

GARY ALLEN

Born in 1959 in Ballymena, County Antrim. His poetry and short fiction has been published widely in literary journals such as the Edinburgh Review and Leviathan. His selection of poetry 'Languages' appeared from Flambard/Black Mountain in 2002.

First Love

In my house, chairs stood against the windows:
I sweated in fear of the man
with a pillow-case over his head.

The night I walked you home,
lads smoking in the shadows
at the gates of the Parochial House –

Go no farther love, you whispered:

a fool youth, in my rut I would have kissed
you under the famine wall.

And my father sprung up
from the locks he was mending
pressing the blade of a screwdriver to my throat,

his eyes burning like Abraham's.

Love changes nothing, you said,
not even bales of shorn hair,
hillocks of broken teeth.

Linen

My grandmother started in the spinning room
when she was eleven years old,
suffered badly from the odour of oil and flax.

Under the North light from the saw-edged roof
she worked from six-thirty to six,
the floors vibrating as the heavy shuttles
thundered across the power looms.

And the excessive temperature, spray from the spindles
the deafening noise from whirling power belts
clashing Jacquard cards, banging sleys.

Young boys spitting up blood
after combing the tow from the line,
and the stink of yarn
dressed with carrageen moss, flour and tallow.

You had to be quick on the whistle
to doff bobbins of spun yarn on oiled flyers,
or a whack with a rod across the knuckles.

When she got an infection
from standing bare-foot in the contaminated water,
they had to wrench out the entire root
of the great toe-nail, leaving her with a limp.

And a best friend who fainted with hunger
had her hair entangled in the carding machinery -
lost the greater part of her scalp.

Now they are knocking the old building down
the iron ball turning the small brick to dust,
and I remember as a child, how on passing
she always spat at the chained gate.

Sisyphus

I first tasted stone as a child,
carrying club-money in the wrong estate.

Brought up in the truth,
I gave my religion in innocence.

Stone is never forgotten,
the selection and the throwing is ritual

with the breaking of bone, the cutting of hair:
we love the death we have given.

Those women on the Maiden City wall
hurling stone at history

were only responding to fear.

It is how we fall,
the thickness of a coin.

In that Mexican summer
while others sweltered by television-sets,

I dribbled round
the husks of burning cars

marking myself for persecution
by gracing the only house with broken windows.

Fire-Watcher

The narrow-gauge is gone:
buckets hang from the sky
on rusted pulleys

mud tracks lead through trees
to tumbled stones,

and dog nails litter the forest floor.

I am an iron man in red skin,
I'll eat and drink this strange earth too.

Up here on the watch-tower
I search out fire among the mines,

and Rathlin looks like a girl
sleeping on a restless sea.

For men whose eyes are blind to separation,
I listen to the wind alone
far above water, plantation, Belfast skyline:

the squeal of wagons long gone to scrap.

You iron buckets,
let me ride you one last time
crashing through the dripping pine-tops

like the white horse foaming
over Ess-na-Larach

down to the disused Red Bay pier
and the history that is me.

The Workhouse

My great grandmother tended the sick
comforted the dying
with the only medicine she had –
words from the bible.

She laid-out the dead
washing the bruised limbs, encrusted sores
of cadavers already skeleton,
boxed waxen-faced infants

and delivered orphans
from girls too young and weak
in the same sulphurated room.

Said the greatest fear of the old
was not death
but the pauper's grave, no headstone.

Families waited in the winter cold
to bring bundles on sticks
under the cover of darkness

and men laid roads through pine forests,
over bogland, that pestered out
on some inaccessible hill.

On her death-bed she recited names,
desolated parishes.

And here am I, cutting out dry-rot
under the roof of a listed building
uncovering impoverished prayers
scratched into overhead beams

neighbours, family, friends,
remembered only by what they have hidden –
faded ribbon, bow, glass beads, lock of hair.

Early Morning, North Antrim

This is how it must have been in the beginning,
the first grey light of the morning
coming through the clouds at sea

and no sound other than the suddenness of water
rushing up rock channels, onto the shore.

We no longer see anymore the primitive
in our lives: this is what early man looked on

and understood the nature of things,
the gouged out glen under Torr Head,
the vulnerability of the dawn coastline.

The spume on our bare hands and feet,
the cockle, limpet, crab
is the same salt and meat they tasted.

So what if regimented firs
cover the escarped sides of Orra More
instead of Hazel, Oak, Scotch Pines?
they are only given names.

Nothing has fundamentally changed –
we sense the same instinctive fear
understand the ritual of flesh
bones placed in souterrains.

The Brick Factory

Another man's child is our enemy,
stealing bread from the mouths of the unborn
fetid air from the slums.

These are our forefathers -
children with clay hands, clay faces,
already old in the brick fields.

Bare feet walk the hard mud lanes
with bottles of tepid water, heel of loaf,
always keeping the chimney-stack in view.

This is a festival of labour:
lines of brick drying in the sun
bunting hanging from traction-engines.

And down by the duckweed, marsh-marigolds,
a threadbare lay-preacher shouts,
Hardship is redemption and hope sin.

Cromwell came this way too
left his dead covered with bramble
and his mark deeper than chiselled stone.

And whose gene-pool ended on the side of Tuftarney Hill?
a mile's drag from the narrow-gauge railway
and the quarry-pits, delicate head bricked-in.

It's the eyes we remember, the scorn,
as if being born in some other time or place
could free any of us.

JOHN O'DONNELL

John O'Donnell was born in 1960. He won the Hennessy/Sunday Tribune New Irish Writing Award for Poetry in 1998. In 2001 he won The Ireland Funds Listowel Writers' Week Prizes for Best Individual Poem and Best Short Collection. He has also twice been runner-up in the Patrick Kavanagh Poetry Competition. His first full-length collection, 'Icarus Sees His Father Fly', will be published by Dedalus in 2003.

The Shipping Forecast

Tied up at the pier in darkened harbour
the two of us below, in cabin's amber
light; me surly in a sleeping-bag, fifteen,
and you, past midnight, calmly tuning in
to the Shipping Forecast, long wave's
crackle, hiss, until you find the voice.
What's next for us: rain or fair? There are
warnings of gales in Rockall and Finisterre.
So near now, just this teak bulkhead
between us, and yet so apart, battened
hatches as another low approaches, the high
over Azores as distant as a man is from a boy.
I think of my own boat one day, the deep.
Beside me the sea snores, turns over in its sleep.

Christmas 1914

Dawn. On either side they lean
against each other, shivering
inside greatcoats that don't fit. In
ink-blue air they finger
keepsakes, scribble final letters home
and wait for the command.
And someone sweetly punts
a football into no-man's land.

Who started this? I'd have loved to meet
the man for whom the whole world
was the certainty of stitched leather
at his feet. No notion, surely, of the rights
of smaller nations as he packed it in
among the extra socks and cartridge
belts; all he'd seen then were coats
piled up for goalposts, picking teams,

and the usual arguments about
what crossed the line, or didn't
in the end. Now for once the dream
is real as soldiers step from dugouts
and from trenches, wary of this eerie
dress rehearsal until the space is gradually
filled with shouts pluming the air,
frosted ridges crunching underfoot,

the hoofed ball rising high and falling
back, then booted once again into
the middle distance. What is there left
between them except swapped cigarettes,
swigs of vodka and of rum? For hours
afterwards they sit around, learning

new card games, the airs of old sad songs
they still hum as they part, with sheepish hugs

and promises to return. One by one
they disappear, fading into dusk.
Like distant tears the first stars gleam,
as if they know that even after all of this
everything will be different yet the same,
that soon the rats will dart once more
like pickpockets among the dead.
Now evening falls in a swoon

over villages and silent farms that dream
of summer, over the frozen soulless sea,
and over streets in cities on the edge
of history, where boys are still playing
in a dying light, shrieking as they thump
the brand new football plucked
with delighted cries that morning
from under the winking tree.

Missing Persons

Such heartbreak in each grainy photograph
the family has tearfully supplied.
What intimacy these blurred moments have,

squinting into holiday sunlight
or laughing in the pub before the dance.
We can almost feel the weight

of what has happened as we glance
and then move on, a little guiltily,
past this inference of absence

that already we well know
we'll never miss, just faces
in the supermarket queue

or waiting at the bus-stop for a bus
in the dusk of urban evening,
so long as it isn't one of us

who disappears without ever really leaving
in between the shadows and the light;
an ending we hardly can believe in,

the cluttered bedroom quiet
as police teams drag the rivers
and comb the undergrowth, nothing left

except these souvenirs. Clothes
in wardrobes, ghosts on hangers.
A hairbrush full of hairs.

The Match
in memoriam J.F.
for Paddy

The doors and boot banged shut, the engine not
yet started and you'd be switching on. *"He hits it
long again"*; how many Sundays did we hear
a high ball arcing through a summer sky before

being plucked out and belted back into the maw
of our car, among chocolate stains and crisps, more
toothsome fizz-filled drinks than we could finish?
"A right shemozzle here", O'Hehir in the Yiddish

screeching with excitement, my young brother and I
trading pinch for pinch in the back seat as we
headed for the shore, hoping the rain would finally get bored
with us, drift off to ruin someone else's day. You'd

always drive, though you were nowhere near
the spattered windscreen. Eyes fixed in a beatific stare
beyond Strand Road, the seagulls hanging round like knives;
all you could see were goals and points and wides,

Micheàl's frenzied commentary yammering non-stop
from the speaker. Even when you'd park you'd keep
the spell, carrying a transistor over still-damp sand,
a tabernacle tuned in to Athlone, the same one I'd

collected after from the hospital, with the rest of your things.
I'm turning the dial now, following the wave-bands
in case I'd find you. But the only sound I hear is the soft hiss
of the sea. In the end you bowed your head, the way you'd always

done at Mass, but on those Sunday afternoons gave thanks and
praise for hurling and football; me a sherpa stumbling behind,
lugging bathtowels and a deckchair as you strode ahead to join
the congregation, stretched out beside battered radios along

the beach or in the dunes until *"The final whistle"*, tinny cheers
of far-off crowds rising above us like hosannas in the air.

This Afternoon
Omagh, 15 August 1998

In Lingerie she is fingering a nightdress she might wear,
her two bridesmaids to-be skitting beside her. Elsewhere

schoolboys like disgruntled sheep wait in huddles
to be measured up for uniforms, dreaming of girls

and football, a new season this afternoon as summer ends
diminuendo in the town. Here is a father waiting for his sons,

a baby cooing in her pram, and two women browsing for a gift
as shopworkers count the hours down, not long left

till Saturday night, home or out for a few jars,
the raised TV set showing highlights in the bar

of games played earlier today by scrawny heroes
the whole world at their feet, not much older

than the two who've just now parked the car, discreet
that in a moment will bring them all together in the street.

What The Tide Brings In

A wounded star. Crabs in battle-dress.
Salt chorus of a thousand shells. Slumped
blancmange of jellyfish on ochre beach.
A slatted crate that once held oranges. A ball
kicked brightly out of reach. Whale songs.
Kitchen suds. Bladderwrack laid out
in Sunday duds. A ribboned hat,
sunny gust from First Class Deck.
An unnamed bundle in a fertiliser sack.

ADRIAN FOX

Born in 1961, his poems have been widely published. A pamphlet 'Hide Dada, Hide' was published by Lapwing and Simon & Schuster published one of his essays based on his childhood in North Belfast. Some of his work has been recorded by the band Inchequin one of which was a finalist in the national song contest for peace in Cork. A full collection of poetry, 'Surrounded by Sea', will be published by Salmon in 2003.

New York 2001: Fragment

Gazing into the ether's crystal ball,
Sky and a sky, and sky, till death-
My heart stops... Robert Lowell.

I woke at six this morning, disturbed
By one of those dreams of falling
Where, they say if you don't wake up
Before you hit the ground, you're dead.

The images splintered away festering
Like a slither of metal or glass imploding
Beneath the cornea of my eye.

I was falling with others filling the sky
Then I was watching them fall grey,
Ashen, dust, a flimsy hologram.

The dew that flies
Suicidal, at one with the drive
into the red
Eye, cauldron of morning.

I'm trying to assemble these words
From the debris of Sky News, poems'

By Robert Lowell, Sylvia Plath
And a dictionary to look up "Ether",
Only to find a line from "Paradise Lost".

Him, the almighty power hurled
Headlong from the ethereal sky.

I recalled being the son of a terrorist
In Belfast, I picked up half a brick
And watched it take to the air, kite like
Swimming, until it crashed into the face
Of a black British soldier.

I didn't know then that I was the Siegfried
Sassoon of Ardoyne. I didn't want a slap
On the back to congratulate the fine shot
Or another X marked in my school jotter
That replaced the teachers star.

This was war and I was sick to death of it.

I ran like the blood trickling along his face
Through the crevices and alley-ways
Into a friend's intestines slithering like
Snails on the concrete. His mother yelling
"The bastards have shot my only son".

That night I cried myself to sleep
And lost myself in a peaceful dream.
It seems I have to go back there into
The dark recesses of my childhood
To let the words come out the other side.

Can you run away through the Avenues
Of blood, a friend or family member's
Image flickering when you close your eyes?
Can you wake in the morning and refuse
The X being marked on your school jotter?

Half A Sestina For Stephanie

How can I write a sestina for you
Six stanzas of six lines concluding death,
Killing yourself in a three line envoy.
I, who doesn't know the time of day
When the lines of your life were diverted
To lie low in the Blue-stoned soil.

Reliving grief, my hands delve in the soil
Moulding a clay figurine of you.
Retracing the black paths that diverts
My gaze away from the sunset to death.
A photograph of you on your wedding day
Your smile didn't convey love's envoy.

Was it back then that the messenger
Whispered phlegmed words that soiled
Your soul to fall early to your funeral day.
Did a touch reach out and abuse you
Fondling filthy caresses to die
Out there on the back roads where diverted

Diversions took you round and round
To fall foul of the dead end.

Radio Realism

On the little teak Marconi
In the attic space of 73 Etna Drive
We watched Match of the Day.
The bunk beds now separated sounded
Like a football supporter's rattle.
Beside the tower of cards on the chest
Of drawers between us were two sets
Of 11 perfectly placed, Manchester United
And Tottenham Hotspur.

When the black and white images faded
Into God save the queen and the white
Dot on the TV disappeared.

The images were replaced by the frantic
Crackle of police messages echoing signals
From the street through the dormer window.
Megahertz igniting Molotov cocktails
And the inferno of Farringdon Gardens.
Unlike "The War of the Worlds" the black
Screen transmitted a special powers act,
Roger, Charlie, Victor and Bravo
Brought the front door down.

The Light On The Stones

I retrace your final journey now in a blue car,
Not black, alone on the motorway.
Passing the Maze prison the stench of my engine
Overheating is like gunpowder, spent shells,
Lingering, your dream of Irish freedom.

I climbed the mountain graveyard
Above the violent divided city,
Above the peaceline that stood between us
In the living room. It was a maze
Of kept graves, lawns, wreaths, flowers,
Names on glistening headstones.

Your plot all weeds,
And wild grass cries out for order.
The fallen wooden cross bears no name;
But you are there. Like a sculptor
With clay I reach inward, my hands
As delicate as salmon wings riding
The white water, struggling
The strong currents of grief.

I brush the soiled tears from your eyes
And you wake in me, swimming
And glistening in mine. My hands
Shape the clay moulding our wounded past,
Emerging in the light on the stones.

Wait for me to lie down on the grass, on the weeds
On the boulder you rest your head upon.

A Tricolour In Tatters

On the apex of a house
just across the road
A tricolour in tatters.

It wasn't it's vibrant colours
That caught my eye, but
The grey November sky
Flickering through the torn green.

It looks like it's been there
Since nineteen sixty nine.

The orange flaps and scrapes
Along the harsh roof tiles.
The white is just a long string

Hanging on by the skin
Of symbolic peace, half mast
On a bent rusting pole.

Blue

The harbour wall
Holds the fishermen
In a stone embrace,
Like naked lovers
Embedded in the sand.
Hands grip the rod
The tourniquet.
The captured one
Struggles, dragged
From aquamarine.
The crack of flesh
On concrete, sapping
The earth, the sea,
The last flickering
Colour grey, steel,
Hate, prize.
The swishing
Swirl of casting
Lines shiver Blue.

CHERRY SMYTH

BORN IN 1961, GREW UP IN PORTSTEWART AND LIVES IN LONDON. HER DEBUT COLLECTION, 'WHEN THE LIGHTS GO UP', LAGAN PRESS, WAS PUBLISHED IN 2001. HER POETRY WON PRIZES IN THE LONDON WRITERS COMPETITION AND CARDIFF INTERNATIONAL. SHE EDITED 'A STRONG VOICE IN A SMALL SPACE', A COLLECTION OF WOMEN'S PRISON POETRY, CHERRY PICKING PRESS, 2002. HER SHORT FICTION HAS APPEARED IN SEVERAL ANTHOLOGIES, INCLUDING 'THE ANCHOR BOOK OF NEW IRISH WRITING', 2000.

Human Image

I am looking at a painting by Louis le Brocquy
of a finger-hole poked in wet cement.
Slowly, a wounded, receding face appears,
a grey mirage of head, holding the spirit captive.
The hole fastens into a mouth,
taut as a navel, screaming.

We waited for the images on television
to resolve into fiction. We watched blazing
pieces shower down the column of eyes,
kept watching until belief occurred,
somewhere behind the retina where
incomprehension burnt a dark hole.

How to carry the bulk and heft of it - this new way
to think about dying. We would anticipate
smithereens in the North, take the risk of living,
not without regard, but unguarded, attentive,
summoning forgiveness from a gap of light,
a place that could not be set in stone.

In Residence

They come in clutches with remnants of paper,
creased and tucked. Rubbish to anyone else
but alive and beating as a chick to them.
Some I must gentle into my palm,
others hunt me down for a trophy.

The rhythm is early childhood,
the tick tock of the first clock,
the singsong of a group verse,
words long forgotten
but the strokes reliable as chocolate.

There's not much I can give except to say well done,
make a strong voice in a small space.

Sometimes their glee is four years old,
wild, susceptible and bright. It carries them like swifts
bearing gifts that will attend to the source.
Nested words, a small crown, soft lined,
something to hold their head up for.

On bad days, their eyes are nerveless, screened.
They don't preen. Only strip-light can enter.
They've taken poison and I watch
as they tear their words into
small white pieces for the birds.

In The South That Winter

We both went a little crazy in the South that winter
and now we can admit it, now that it's over
and we've come through and I'm crossing the Hudson on a train.
I remember running from our bed to lie on the wee bed
in the study, in a sleeping bag, which smelt of sand
and dust and someone else's sleep,
and beating it on my thighs till feathers
broke loose and my cries were white.
You tried to stop me, frightened by the sounds I made,
your hands placed where anger would not place them.
You must have wanted to show blood
for you smashed the beloved, shipped china cabinet,
and tore up the Couple's book I bought to save us.
Pages lay in an intimacy of blood and glass.

We both claimed the most injury.
Boy, does every love contain such hate?
Yet here I am, not fresh as a daisy, more like
a full, fat rose whose petals curl brown at the edges,
but whose stem is thick, a thorned artery deep in the earth,
or a sunflower, clustered with seeds, its dishevelled head,
a little heavy after a blistering summer in full field.
For you, the day after, fist bandaged, had dragged
garden furniture on to the beach before I got up,
made breakfast and led me to the water,
to sit and eat in the light with you, like queens,
perfectly calm and perfectly happy.
People walking past could see how in love we were
and wanted a place at our white table.

The End Of July

The end of July, bunting bullied
by the east wind. A German camper van
on the narrow road ahead –
a sign some things have changed.
My father drives with erratic caution,
blasting the horn at each sharp-hedged bend.
I hear my sister's voice from childhood,
'Don't be silly, Daddy,
the hedges won't move!'

The red, the white, the blue curbstones
won't budge either and it's a relief to take
the coast road to Cushendall.
The sea is limpid, full of vanishing.
A red trawler hangs in glassy nothingness,
its engine throbbing.

We wind down to Murlough Bay,
walk to the small cove.
'The McLachlans owned that place,'
Dad points to the cottage on the shore.
'Would you be McLachlans?'
he asks a passing couple,
the woman's hair, illuminated tangerine.
'Oh no,' she says, 'we're only down for the day.'
'To watch the birds.'
We all look out to sea and commend the calm.
We say goodbye, watch them walk back.
'People,' my father says, 'are all right
when you speak to them.'
'Yes', I answer, wondering what itch of prejudice
framed his view.
'Does she dye her hair?' he asks suddenly.

'Definitely,' I laugh.

He's learnt to suss everything is not as it seems.
I tell him of the night before in a crowded bar,
when a flute-player struck up The Sash
and half the place joined in. One young woman
caught my eye, my closed lips and winked,
'Sure I only learnt it to get past the Prods.'

My father and I decipher Scotland, say little.
We're not a family to name sea campion,
thift, mont bretia, I've learnt all that since,
from books, but he can tell a buzzard treading
air overhead and stretches out his fingers
to form wing tips.

He hands me a smoothed round
of basalt, hot with inward heat
drawn from a sun behind thin cloud.
It stays warm until we reach the car.
I know it will become his worry stone,
hope it stores the best of this afternoon –
the seeping milky light, water and sky as one,
all division illusory.

'hot with inward heat' is the name of an Eilis O'Connell sculpture, 1990

The Roadside

The killer is a country man, close to land
his father's father's father fought to keep.
He weaves his tractor up and down thin fields,
hedged with secrets and mutters tenderly
to pigs and sheep.

He knew Brennan at St. Malachy's,
a snitch even then – courted his sister
who married a teacher – they thrashed conkers
on laces, raced three-legged on Sport's Day
and won a sixpence.

It is midsummer and the farmer longs for dark.
The etiquette of execution sharply honed
keeps silence chain-smoked in the carpark.

Brennan is bull-drunk, taken easy, stripped and baled.
His Guinness-gut shivers, pale as potato.
The killer milks him slow, then twists his balls
until he yelps and bleats, like all beasts
out in sweet June air, for Eileen O'Neill,
shot and bargained away at twenty-six.

Brennan's voice is calm now, as one who knows
he is already dead. One letter for the wife.
Claire. Seven months pregnant. For pity's sake.

The sister is somewhere in his face.
The farmer bends.
There is nothing in the barn
only a ripped paper bag and biro
stamped with Lurgan Motors.

Shit-smell of Brennan
is stronger than manure
and in his eyes
the slaughter-look of calves,
so when he writes,
the killer needs to kill,
to bag the head, mow him down, plough
until he squeals no more.

The farmer carts the body to a quiet road
and slips on home, past swollen sacks of silage.
Later he will muck out the boot of his Sierra,
daylight clinging to his hands.

Water

is where I'm happiest,
naked, if possible, out of my depth,
my breasts going their own way,
cracks rinsed and explored,
like it's a given, a marriage
where no asking is necessary.

I dive under, hair growing ecstatic,
frondish, slower to turn back than
my head, limbs unhumiliated, strong,
feet playful. More efficient than walking,
I front crawl, breath timed, pronounced,
not slipping by unnoticed.
This is alive!

Then comes floating,
skin a guest of air.
I hold my palms just beneath
the surface, plying the tension
as if they could lift the water up
and it would not break, like love should be,
elastic, fluent, so familiar,
you can't tell if you're in it or out of it.

KATHERINE DUFFY

BORN IN DUNDALK IN 1962, AND NOW LIVES IN DUBLIN WHERE SHE WORKS AS A TRANSLATOR IN THE HOUSES OF THE OIREACHTAS. HER POETRY COLLECTION 'THE ERRATIC BEHAVIOUR OF TIDES' WAS PUBLISHED BY THE DEDALUS PRESS IN 1999. SHE ALSO WRITES FICTION; HER AWARD-WINNING IRISH-LANGUAGE NOVEL FOR TEENAGERS 'SPLANCTHA!' WAS PUBLISHED BY CLÓ IAR-CHONNACHTA IN 1997, AND HER SHORT STORIES IN ENGLISH HAVE BEEN SHORTLISTED FOR HENNESSY LITERARY AWARDS.

Season

Working in the factory, we made
light of the large tobacco-leaves,
bundles of jungle, stacked to grow
blonde and brittle, fit to be shredded. We
worked much further down the line
in Packing. Boxes cool with cellophane flew,
monotonously expert, from our hands.

Autumn came, and I slunk away,
and left you plotting marriage among
the gold leaves, the boxes, the machines,
my stint as Carmen at an end; it still

sings to me, at times. Evenings
we drank lager, smoked for free,
and dressed with a wild precision;
our skirts the colours of sunlight,
of stirred blood, of trees, our earrings
moving like tavern signs. Our heels were
high and thin, and deft as knives.

Bilingual

A woman with turf on her hands
asks a question of her son;
he replies in a different tongue,
inquires can he borrow the car
to go to the disco, along
stark roads where she once heard
sounds of the fairies' churning,
odd syllables, turned to water now
in grassy gutters, by light's
expert reductionism.

She sighs, and he prepares
with strongly-worded aftershave,
in the corner of the built-on
bathroom where tides recede.

Planet DIY

Wishing to redecorate our lives,
on Sunday afternoons we visit
Planet DIY,
stopping off at its most hopeful places,
Tile City, Carpetland, The World of Beds...

where couples
finger lampshades longingly, and cast
fierce glances on furniture.
The planet's atmosphere
is thin with wishfulness,

its language intricate, precise;
ceiling rose, dado-rail, shower-head,
we mutter in the endless aisles

where paintcard shades
ply their deceitful spectrum
Desert Wind, Pale Dawn, Frozen Lake,

a gloss of spacious adventure
we are unlikely now to know.
Our adventure will be
to make love beneath the perfect headboard
imperfectly.

We're conversant in the planetary skills
pasting, priming, sanding, grouting.
Our lives are empty rooms. What colours
will we paint them?

Transaction

Give us your heart, they said,
we'll hang it in a different cage,
and you can have what you want.
It's collateral, you see,
a red jewel, glistening; besides,
it's irregular throbbing amuses us.
Give it here, we'll grant you each comfort
up to, and including, central heating.
Now my heart's a high parrot, calling
whatever they want it to say,
and, in an empty chest, I keep
all that it might have wished for.

Fuschia City
(West Cork)

I've come here to be alone
but there's a city of insects in the fuchsia.
Flies are browsing in its dark boutiques
moaning at the prices of the harlequin gowns.
Bees drink their brains out in showy emporia
then drone blues tunes 'bout how their queen
just don't appreciate them anymore.

In the leaves' multi-storeyed aerodromes
a tight schedule of arrivals and departures
operates – each second someone's taking off
or coptering down. I've come here for some peace,
but those manic, stressed-out insects
keep whispering and muttering in my ear,

fretting they'll be late for the butterfly ballet,
bitten by the knowledge that paralysis, extermination
is just a swat, an acrid spray away;
it's a risk no health insurance policy will cover...
I've come here to be idle but, unwittingly,
I've built a city of insects in the fuchsia.

Bubblewrapped

We are flirting with death by travel again,
closing our ears to what could be done,
looking away when the stewardess
makes her pantomime.

We have been to a sculptured city.
Its towers are packed in our hearts,
and in boxes, spoils of the market,
crystal, bubblewrapped.

Plusher cells coddle
the skeleton's dance by the Town Hall clock,
the unpronounceable streets,
the mulled wine we drank…

Death lets us off, but the baggage is late;
we assume the various shapes of waiting,
annoyed at finding this small torture
at the thin end of our adventure.

We're eyeing each other resentfully
when, with a shudder, the carousel starts,
and we make away, hands full, hearts
blown and stretched as glass.

Restorers Versus The Ceiling Vandal

You can stipple all you like,
I know the cracks are there,
lithe, expressive. I still see

the small boat splinter
on the wiry waterfall,
the pound of butter melt,
martyred, in marvellous light,
the crow's foot – trident
of the laughing ceiling eye,
its iris one unquenchable
damp spot...

          Stipple away!
thinking you'll make my ceiling calm
and whole, and give to years
of insomniac tracery
the stiff consistency
of solid citizenship.

It's all right, because I know
that at night, when outside,
cars sidle and stop,

jagged razors of light will come
floating over the curtain-tops
to cut your ceiling to shreds.

I'll lie and watch
the scars proliferate.

DAMIAN SMYTH

Born in Downpatrick, Co Down, in 1962. His debut volume, 'Downpatrick Races' (Lagan Press), appeared in 2000. A stage play, 'Soldiers of the Queen', an epic set in the Boer War, will premiere in October 2002 in Downpatrick and then to the Belfast Festival at Queen's and on tour. A second collection of poems, 'The Down Recorder', is due in the winter of 2002.

The Mighty Arkle
bay gelding by Archive out of Bright Cherry

The horse bought fridges, TVs, motor cars.
It was no wonder thousands gripped the rails
when the hero hunted Millhouse down again,
pulling back the earth with each great stride,

the pride of England frothing, broken, bate.
If I had a cap, I'd throw it in the air.
This was how the Irish won the war,
everything riding on every whipping boy

to face the white man down against the odds.
I have my grandda's photo of the god,
an icon, like good Pope John and JFK,
Pat Taaffe up, who, he used to say,

needed that horse 'for he couldn't sit on a stool'.
But the beefcake underneath is Cassius Clay,
the footwork perfect, the arrogance a joy,
the sucker punch a lucky horseshoe in each glove.

Inside

The night the cages caught fire in Long Kesh
and the camp went down with its lights on like the Titanic,
soldiers cleared the screws out of the wings in Crumlin Gaol
and beat the fuck out of my brother.

John Henry turned things upside down for Ireland,
for side-burns, bell-bottoms and thruppenny bits,
the years between Slade and the Sex Pistols spent
rinsing and spitting a mouthful of cracked teeth

and turning out cotton hankies embroidered with felt-tip,
of which a simple touch would send a stain spreading
like a sunburst indelibly down to the tiniest filigree.
Old Aggie Breen with no teeth, opening her son's clothes parcel

and finding inside his shirt tattooed with blood,
kept it in the hot press exactly as it was,
bringing it out as needs be, a relic for strangers,
the baffled hurt of years congealed in her homespun heart.

And John Henry put his skill at metalwork to good use,
fashioning a celtic ring from a 50-pence coin,
so turned inside itself that the Queen's head vanished,
Fidei *Defensor* impossibly on the inside rim.

Imagine Belfast

Mrs. Carmody
an Irish woman
who could tell a story
when she'd a bit taken

William Carlos Williams, last fragment of Paterson, Book VI (1961)

I   1935
How incongruous it is.
My father on a train
at the age of eight,
the carriages shivering
along the rails
all the way from the Loop,
from Lecale to the city,
to Ballymacarrett,
to Moira Street
which is not there,
an envelope for his granny's son
held somewhere safe,
out of the road
so no one would notice.
'Put you this into his hand,
no one else's.'

II   1945
"Eighteen people were killed and more than forty injured this morning in one of the most appalling disasters of Northern Ireland railway history which occurred on the Belfast and Co Down line when the 7.40 rail car from Holywood crashed into the rear of the 7.10 workmen's train from Bangor ...
The rear carriage of the Bangor train, packed with workmen, some of whom were standing, was smashed to matchwood when the railcar,

travelling at not more than 10 miles an hour, sliced its way through the
end coach of the stationary train."

III   1900
George Linton put his head down at Hart's Hill
and never lifted it. He's found there still,

cinders smouldering under the Boer dust
for a hundred years, young, unnatural, at rest.

His father and brother are bunked at home
out of range of the longest Long Tom,

on their backs up the Killough Road forever,
the two of them hugging the wall, taking cover.

IV   1902
"On Monday 20th January, the workforce reported for duty at the usual time of 6.30am and after the time permitted for their first break disaster struck. At approximately 9.30am an extremely loud crashing sound was heard throughout the mill and moments later it was discovered that a large section of the building had collapsed."

V   1945
Even though he was bleeding from the head,
Guard Hewitt staggered back down the track,
weaving and stumbling between rails and cinders,
to warn the oncoming train from Bangor
that, up ahead, behind him in the dark
the unbearable had already taken place,
that what they had most feared
had come upon them. Blood
and rails and sinew and sleepers,
one body severed in two.

VI

"If any there be which are desirous to be strangers in their owne soile and forrainers in their owne citie they may so continue and therein flatter themselves. For such I have not written these lines and taken these paines."
Camden

VII   1935

It's thirty-five years since the firepower of farmers
cut up his brother and dozens of others.
Now John Linton waits for my father's train
bringing the boy and the notes from his ma.
He'll take him surely by the hand up to North Street
and set him up in the stalls in the Alhambra
(Charlie Chan and Number One Son)
and take himself by the hand to the optics
hanging by the heels at the back of the house.
Big day in the city. The rails lead back home.
The rows of cast steel. The Rose of Castille.

VIII   2002

He's sick in the ambulance.
It rolls and bucks along the back roads,
heading for Belfast. A lost reel from Stagecoach
and that's Death after him, pounding the dust,
whooping and firing through the dusk windows
and he's complaining that there's no shock absorbers
on the old crates they use to carry emergencies.
For a moment, travel sickness is worse than his heart.

IX   1945

"Visibility was very bad. It was pitch black. There was a scramble for the doors and I could hear women scream. Someone had the presence of mind to break up some of the woodwork of the carriages to make a fire and it was by this light that the ambulance men and doctors worked."

X   2002
My father's son is alone in the Royal,
learning what loneliness is from equipment.
The ambulance he hopes is still rushing
is somewhere out on the plains from Downpatrick.
The wind is opening the automatic doors.
Everyone turns. No one comes in.

XI   By Amelia Street
       we sat down and wept.
The prostitutes at the Europa Hotel are cast in bronze,
aere perennius, more lasting than bronze
are the breasts of their pots and pans
and the wide hips of their typewriters and bobbins.

The anonymous mothers and murderers of children,
the young man upstairs hanging by the neck
in north Belfast,
while downstairs the table is laid for his girl
(Your cheatin' heart will make you weep
You'll cry and cry and try to sleep),
the miraculous ballet of a drunk in rush hour
treading an invisible tightrope homeward,
as gormless and cunning as Buster Keaton,
the Chinese restaurant burnt out by thugs,
prawn crackers popping and crackling for hours
and everywhere the ghosts of 300 years
in caps and shawls and redcoats and bad boots,
the millies crushed in the Pipe Lane collapse,
the bodies of the Blitz stacked up like turf
in the hold of the Falls municipal pool,
dead policemen, dead daughters, dead soldiers
of one cause or another, of every cause
from the Princess Victoria to HMP Maidstone,
the Clyde Valley packed to the gunwales with guns,
to the oil rigs striding like Gulliver forever

out to the North Sea, up to their knees in ink.

XII   1902
"The collapse of the portion of the mill was due to [a] defect at the base of the piers and we are of the opinion that the defect could not have been discovered by ordinary inspection, and that no blame can be attached to any person in connection with the accident."

XIII   2002
Anaesthetic Breathing Systems
Anaesthetic Catheter Mounts
Yankeur Suction Catheters
Trachea Tubes
Nasopharyngeal Airways
Sytlet/Introducers
Peritoneal Lavage Sets
Defib Pads
Tymp Genius Probe Covers
Portable Sphygmos
Arubu Face Masks
Chest Drain Equipment
Trocar Catheters
Drainage Tubing Sets
Warm Air Blankets
Wool Balls
Disposable Suction Liners
Vacuum Splints
Stoma Flange & Bags
Astrup/Blood Gas
20000ml Portex Bottles
Diathermy/High Temperature Cautery

XIV   1902
Ellen Scott (14), 4 Letitia Street, doffer; Alice Cunningham(20), 17 Jude Street, reeler; Mary Burns (18), 34 California Street, spinner; Mary Burke (19), 39 Arnon Street, spinner; Mary Kerr (20), 9 Union

Street, spinner; Annie Hunter (16), 8 Sackville Street, doffer; Mrs Davidson (50), unknown, reeler; Mary Williamson (22), 68 Gulian Street, spinner; Ellen Corr (40), 14 Artillery Street, preparer; Alice McDonnell (18), 4 Linton Street, preparer; Mary Duff (60), 23 Wilson Street, reeler; Lizzie Campbell (20), 117 Bristol Street, reeler; Martha McAuley (13), 39 Wall Street, doffer.

XV
Of those is our culture. Of those is our art.
No one forgotten. Nothing escapes.
Thousands of Protestants shipped in by Citybus
to the centre of a city that's yours and yours,
solemn and silent in their Sunday best,
and a Catholic glacier of black flags carving the Falls ...
the people are moving, migrating, shifting,
incorrigible, indiscreet and in public,
never having learnt to suffer in silence
or just be content with shaking fists at a screen.

Get out on the streets and make the dogs bark
and the lights go on in the early morning
and let children stay up late for the fireworks.
'It's a murder picture, that's what it is', after all.
Shop's shut. War's over. No beaten docket.

And, everywhere, Life in spite of ourselves,
because of ourselves, because in Belfast
trouble's no novelty, it's no odds to us
for here's what's worse: we mean what we say
and we'll make everything happen anyway.

XVI   2002
Under fire for 20 years,
fusillades, salvoes, shells,
and every one a bull's-eye,
rocking the shelters,

shaking the plaster
off the arteries,
a shower of shrapnel,
a Long Tom on every hill
lobbing the big steel down
into the valley of my father.

XVII
'Put you this into his hand,
no one else's.'

XVIII 1945
"The Coroner had said that the dead were mourned. They were deeply mourned and something more than that. He understood that all of them, or the greater part of them, were workers engaged in work of national importance who rose at that early hour of the morning to go to their war work, and, therefore, in one sense could it not be said that they were killed in the performance of their national duty, as good Britishers, as good Ulstermen."

XIX 1900
'My brave Irish,' said the Queen
reading the telegrams.
And when the telegrams reached London,
he was still lying, untended,
out on the hillside.

PAULA CUNNINGHAM

Born in Omagh in 1963. A former member of Queen's writers' group, she was awarded an Arts Council grant in 2000. Her poetry chapbook 'A Dog Called Chance' was published in 1999. A monologue, 'The Silver Wake' was performed as part of Tinderbox's programme in 2000; her first radio play, co-written with Mark Illis was broadcast by the B.B.C. this year. She is currently completing her first full collection and also writing prose fiction.

Losing The Keys

Losing the keys I'm at a loss again
though I lock myself out in all weathers
it would appear I specialise in grey skies, rain.

Losing the keys or dreading losing them
it's all the same, the art of losing being
well established in my head,

I set my mind on damage limitation, spares
buried in flowerbeds, lodged with friends; I don
bright gortex, carry an umbrella like a prayer.

But worse than being stranded on your own
doorstep in rain is getting in, no sweat, let's say
a sunny day, chubbing the door, putting on

the chain, losing the keys inside the house
sitting indoors outside yourself again.

Collage

At the turn of the stairs,
the white and turquoise bathroom.
Above the sink
bright fish cavort
in my pink underworld,
embroidered in Miss Passmore's class,
cut-outs in taffeta and silk
from gowns we'd seen Mum wear
in black and white.

The taps are running,
the mirror's all steamed up.
My mother counts out face-cloths,
one for each of us,
before the shriek goes round
the water's hot
it's hot!

She holds them under the cold tap
wrings them out
there now
that's nice and cool
try that
she lays them on the bottom of the bath,
cool patchwork seats against the white
enamel and the heat
now in you hop

Sometimes Dancing

Advance retreat, the chandeliers
are hot tonight, their cut beads
bend the golden light like tears.

Advance, retreat, pass through, dance home.
Gallop. Swing with your partner. Change.
In her dream she is princess, pale

hair coiled in knots, she's trussed in whalebone,
small breasts thrust to touch the heavy choker
at her throat. Advance, retreat. She's been trained

for this, shoulders back, the particular
angle chin and throat describe, balancing
heavy books she thought were made

for practice, and later Mother's precious plates
from China. Sometimes, dancing, she'll force her eyes
up, back, til over the eyebrows' arch

she sees the golden drops, and the room
spins. She does not see
the men she dances with, though she feigns

attention, smiling. She feels
their hands long after they've passed on.
When she dances with Clara she holds tighter

than she should, pushes herself beyond
giddiness. Leans into her. A little.
Once in her dream, swinging,

their bodies locked together and they flew.
She woke to a crashing of plates, a tangle
of sheets in her narrow bed, the heart galloping.

Aubade

Bring the muse into the kitchen
Walt Whitman

A man is squeezing oranges in my kitchen.
I am down the corridor in bed
and he is squeezing oranges
in my kitchen.
From where I lie
I cannot see
the man
but I've deduced
that he
is squeezing oranges.

There is something tremendously erotic
about a man
squeezing oranges.
What is erotic is the sound.
This man
has found my orange squeezer
without my prompting.
He does not know I know
he's squeezing oranges.

Lying here, listening
to the sound of a man
secretly squeezing oranges
at 1.09 of a Sunday afternoon,
I am struck by the fact
that I've never heard any sound
quite so erotic
as the sound of a man
squeezing oranges.

Mother's Pride

Handy with a knife,
His preferred medium
was Mother's Pride plain toast.
This is the way the nuns

eat — soldiers;
this is the Protestant
half. Here's Omagh, Belfast,
Enniskillen, Dublin, Donegal

with Errigal hastily moulded
from Clew Bay, a crumb
for an island for every day
of the year, and Cork,

where John Mac lives.
Lough Erne's two narrow slits;
Lough Neagh his index
finger poked right through.

A final flourish, grinning,
his *pièce de la resistance*
was the border
which my frowning mother

quickly buttered over,
stabbing the bread
and drawing
the knife out clean.

Seeing Things

At the Winter Park ski-holiday reunion
who swans in only Stevie
whose legs don't take him far
– he'd been tinkering under a car
when the bomb went off.

Answer: the skin.
It's Trivia night
and we're in with a chance.
All the other tables are offering liver.
What is the largest organ in the body?

In Winter Park we're triple-wrapped
in thermals
but he's shirtless:
a sophisticated instrument
of thermo-regulation.

Homoeostasis: the body
is a furnace.
The sweat-glands
and erector pili muscles
co-operate to keep the body cool.

The hypothalmus
is conductor of the body's
secret business;
but skin grafts don't have glands
and scars are bald.

Anyway Stevie has walked
the twenty yards from his special car
and he's wrecked
and his stumps are sore
and we get tore in to the drink

and we all get legless
and everyone in the Welly Bar
(we're only here for the ramps
and we've jumped the queue)
is legless and Stevie has taken his off

all smooth American tan
with the socks and the cool shoes on
and we laugh out loud
at the pretty woman
on stilts who almost

jumps out of her skin
and the plastered people
who swear
they're seeing things
and we know they are.

Winter Park Colorado is home to the U.S. National Ski Centre for the Disabled.

MARY MONTAGUE

BORN IN 1964 IN EDERNEY, CO FERMANAGH. SHE HAS PUBLISHED IN SEVERAL NATIONAL JOURNALS AND INTERNATIONALLY IN CANADA. SHE WAS SELECTED BY POETRY IRELAND AS AN EMERGING WRITER FOR THEIR 2001 INTRODUCTIONS SERIES. HER FIRST COLLECTION, 'BLACK WOLF ON A WHITE PLAIN' WAS PUBLISHED BY SUMMER PALACE PRESS IN 2001. SHE WAS THE RECIPIENT OF AN AWARD FROM THE ARTS COUNCIL OF NORTHERN IRELAND IN THE SPRING OF 2002.

The Shepherdess

In Mayo
my car almost collided
with the outrunners
of a flock of sheep
coming over a rise.
Their shepherd followed–
a boy in his mid-teens,
glaring red hair,
dappled copper skin– a lean
epitome of Irishness, loping
to contain the panicked insurrection.
His eyes flicked to mine,
chin inflecting acknowledgement.
Struggling behind
came his sister, another
Irish cliché, but paler,
fatter, slower. I was shocked
at how obviously adolescence
was ravaging her: her awkward
determined dignity; the mortifying
bounce of her breasts; her turned-away
face. She passed me,

eyes stuck to the ground.
It was several seconds
before I could leave her,
floundering in the wake
of her brother's leadership.

December's Close

The story of the night
is written in the snow.
The paths of the forest
are necklaced with foxprints.
Rosaries of pads record
the patrols: the long famished
strides with the furrow
of tail-tip white-lining
the snowcrust. There must
be scores of foxes in these woods:
tracks parallel and weave,
scissor across, edge up to clumps
to snuffle all chances.
The night was long with several
snowfalls to freshen each alien
coating. A single success is marked
where the surface is bloodied
and scuffed, the prints circle
and scatter. Further on,
a scraping where the kill
was set down for the captor
to gobble and gulp. No fur
or feathers remain, just
a frozen nugget of flesh,
a nail-white square of fat.
One victim enough to fortress
a warm mammalian body
against the petrifying air,
enough to get through
another bitter night
of cold and snow and death.

Afterwards

When it is over
I will come home
to moonrise-yellow tundral bleakness,
the bog-browness glowing
with halogenic infusion,
the shadows crisp,
the woad-black sky
brightening around the well of the moon,
the skin of the birches
ghostly under their dappled capes
and, far off, the inky pines
huddling their cavernous shelter.
I will stand in my openness,
quivering. I will bear them,
their deep-timbred ululations,
their quavering soughs.
I will siren them with all the pathos
of my long exile. I will listen
to their answering silence
before they clamour their greeting
with notes of disbelieving joy.
Then I will watch them bead and bob
over the lip of the nearest horizon.
I will wait for them, for to meet them
would burst the membrane stretched across
the brimming ache of my deliverance.
Against the dark cloak of the hill
I will watch their rapid, time-spinning approach:
the rippling undulations of their strong backs
as they lope unswervingly; the rhythmic
flounce of plumed tails; the missile-steady
poise of fixed heads, the ears forward;
and, nearer, the warm ribbons of tongue,

the amber of their gladdening eyes.
Now they tuck their heads, fold
their ears and crinkle muzzles,
showing the beautiful solid
convexity of nape,
the lume-rimed fur.
As they lollop these last
strides, puppyish and playful,
they make adolescents of us all.
I rush to them and we collide,
chest to chest, jowl to jowl,
black lips drawn back to whine
our pleasure and tongue the roofs
of each other's mouths, taste
the other's sweet returning flesh.
We yip and yowl, squirm our bodies
into a wreath of greeting, then
unravel to stream across the unfolding
tundra, the hunt only just begun.

First Day In Cape Breton

That first day, on our way to Cape North:
the highlands rising like giant loaves;
the tangled jarring release wilderness.
We soared and swooped the highway's undulations
through bewildering boundless forest.
Beyond, the Atlantic floored us, a diamanted
cobalt, tempting us forward. At McKenzie,
a cluster of vehicles, jeeps, campers, cars,
their occupants spilling onto the road, gawking
with technified eyes into the sprucedepths.
You ask if we should stop but we've been
travelling all day. We need to reach our rest.
As I pull around, I see him, driver's side,
striding along a gully, this lanky
enormity eluding his pursuers
right across from where they peer and probe.

Jesus, get the camera! I blurt and you
dive, obedient. I stab the button
for the window, slide the glass all the way
down. He's really there, our first moose, as real
as any cow in a field, those towering
legs bearing his immense earth-brown bulk
from us. I slow the car to match him, one
hand on the wheel, one juggling the camera,
while he refuses to break dignity
with a run, but inclines his bulbous chalice
of velveted antler away, assesses
the trees for a break in their screen.
As I struggle to trap the alien
mountainous slope of his back in the lens,
I hear you mutter: *Jeepers look behind!*

I glance in the mirror to see we've been
spotted: a headlighted cavalcade looms
after us. From the other direction
two more cars appear, slow and pull in, their
drivers jumping manly onto the road.
At that, the moose climbs up the ditch, presses
through a gap, pushes into the ragged
furze of spruce. Now the others have caught us.
A swarm of tourists skelters across our view,
squawking and snapping. A shadow of moose
stares back from behind his native cover.
The first man out of the car opposite
approaches my window, his face transfigured.
Where is he? I point to the curious
hulking form, its lowered head juking
under the branches. The man straightens to scan,
then gasp and click. More of the crowd notice
the animal which turns to lumber and
crash his escape through the densely packed trees.
The people sigh. The man looks back at me,
his face rueful and wondering. His own
silence is all I can answer with. When
he looks away, I glance at you. You nod.
I turn back to the wheel and ease my foot
from the brake. We are the first to move off.

NESSA O'MAHONY

BORN IN DUBLIN IN 1964. HER POETRY HAS APPEARED IN A NUMBER OF IRISH, UK, ITALIAN AND AMERICAN PERIODICALS INCLUDING POETRY IRELAND REVIEW, FORTNIGHT, THE SUNDAY TRIBUNE, AGENDA, IOTA, AND THE ATLANTA REVIEW AND HAS ALSO BEEN BROADCAST BY RTE. HER FIRST COLLECTION OF POEMS, ENTITLED 'BAR TALK', WAS PUBLISHED BY ITALICS PRESS IN FEBRUARY 1999. SHE IS EDITOR OF ELECTRIC ACORN, THE DUBLIN WRITERS' WORKSHOP'S ONLINE LITERARY QUARTERLY, WHICH CAN BE FOUND AT WWW.ACORN.DUBLINWRITERS.ORG.

Fin de Siecle

A tree-top sways,
boughs creaking
beneath the amorous weight.
Wings flap with each thrust,
loins enjoined in feathered fury
of bird made bird.
Tumult over, he departs.
She slopes off, eastwards.

I Ching

You bring the coins, your face an oriental mask
for it is serious what we do here,
under a Greek sky and the purple bougainvillaea.

I have no parchment to record the passing of this day
so a notebook must suffice to transcribe the hexagrams
as I cast and cast again. "They're called yarrow," I say

and you nod briefly, not distracted from the task of divination
as you squint at the shapes drawn, all tanned, purblind gravity
and you begin to read the answer to what I may or may not have asked.

Your voice slows to a crawl of intonation as you incant
of a blue-eyed man who'll lead me cross the river
to a complete harmony of opposites, which do attract, of course.

"That makes sense," I lie, my turn for enigma as I gaze off to the hills,
although I should take my cue from the cockerels here, who know
there is no wrong time and no right time, to be heard.

Valentia Sunset

And after all
the screams and yells
of a million catastrophes,
wars with plastic swords
and light sabres,
the dart that went astray
in the youngest's eye,
countless roars
of territories breached,
and defended,

quietness fell
as the sun dipped
towards the Atlantic,
firing the sky,
silencing us for the instant
that the crow flew
westwards
and the lighthouse
blinked itself awake
to coming night.

Hit Delete

First from the database,
a cursor swipe backwards,
laying blank to syllables
I couldn't pronounce anyway.
Next to the inbox,
your messages a right click away
from obliteration.

I pause, thinking how years ago
I might have gathered them up,
damp from maiden's tears,
and wrapped them, beribboned
into a box destined for dust
and the top shelf.

No, I prefer erasure,
the steely composure
of thumb and index,
as I make my mouse
roar

They're Grand, When You Can Give Them Back
for Anna and Sean Ceroni

So this is what I'm missing out on?
The dawn chorus, the splintering
of a house's sound sleep,
the screams, the wordless refrain
that knows its own tune?
The litany of wants and complaints,
the missing cat, shoe, beaker?
The sand in eyes,
the never letting up throughout a day
of near misses, grazed knees, pulled hair,
balancing acts near precipices?

My involuntary jerk, arms outstretched,
is just a throw-back - my mother's genes reappear
from the time she watched her man on the edge,
a Slea Head drive with five under 10 in the back,
nothing to choose between rock and blue air,
squeezing her eyes shut till it was over.
That was the same trip
that he led us all out to where white paint
dripped its warning on the pier,
my mother the helpless watcher on the shore.

But these pair aren't mine,
and so the urge that overtakes some time
to toss their hair, the jolt of pleasure
if they put a hand in mine on the roadway,
is just an impulse, a jangle of nerve-endings,
a ganglion hot-wired.

Venice Postcards

1. At The Peggy Guggenheim

Riveted by a boy again,
equestrian this time, bronze,
erection pointing canal-wards
sign-posting the end
of this pilgrimage
through a dilettante's garden.
Who wouldn't choose
to be buried with their art
and 14 shih-tzus?

2. Hold The Bellinis

We're suave here,
in Harry's Bar,
sipping insouciance
with Negronis.

A nonna, elegant in furs
has our measure.
She's seen the type before,
sipping the pink fizz,
checking the recipe
in Cadogans.

Windows closed, frosted
to contain our universe,
preserve our pose
against the glint on water,
the shimmering delight
of a palazzo.

3. School Outing

Straight from Grafton Street to the Riva,
voices shrill, dodging dames in furs
as they rush, fuelled by something sneaked
between gondola rides and secret tours.

Panicking mid the tri-corn hats,
clutching bags, fleeing the Carnivale
as they clatter on, dropping cameras,
a compact bought in Boots.

Till they're brought up short,
energy corralled by the gate-keeper
waiting for them at the water's edge
tapping her foot, lips pursed

Santa Salute chimes the lock-up bell.

4. On The Gondola

It might have been romantic
if we'd both brought someone else,
so we settled for self-consciousness,
eyeing Robetro's spiel with Roberto's ass.

No hand trailing here,
but languidness all the same
being propelled through the calle
hearing the water lap, the plop
of plaster crumbling,
a rat swimming somewhere.

KATE NEWMANN

Born in 1965, educated at King's College, Cambridge. She edited 'The Dictionary of Ulster Biography' (1993) while a junior fellow at the Institute of Irish Studies in Queen's University, Belfast. She teaches Creative Writing and co-directs The Summer Palace in South Donegal, where she now lives. Her collection 'The Blind Woman in the Blue House' was published by Summer Palace Press in 2001.

Gabriela Mistral, Nobel Prize Winner

No mystery to her
The passion of skin and abandon;
The indoctrination of light through a high school window,
Its frame rotting.
Lucila Godoy Alcayaga from the Elqui Valley
Took the pennames *Alguien, Soledad, Alma*
Then became Miss Mistral, marshalling her hours
Into hemlines and chalk and restless feet
Singlets and Shakespeare, a door left banging
Down a corridor emptied of children.

Her poems full of truant lust:
A classroom at night, the moon
An echo in the depth of its dogmatic throat;
A pipistrel cry from the eaves,
A mutter of shifting pigeons,
The Aconcagua sky
Deeper than sought-for death;
Stars older than sin,
Inconceivable.

Pablo Neruda's House In Valparaiso

The narrow dance of corridor and cramp;
Crows-nest dreams of foraging in soil.
Above the rummaging heat
It craves the rank slap
Of waves in the working port.
From here the Pacific becomes a map of abstraction,
Etching our unbearable past,
Too wide for words.

Built to take in all of Valparaiso,
La Sebastiana fears the flight of our passerine thoughts,
Watching pigeons – their terrifying white and silver escape
Against hot unwitting Valparaiso blues -
Disappear like swatches of misremembered songs.

It is all too late, too overworked, the cumbersome armchair
Nicknamed *La Nube*, the footstool
Stained with green ink;
The clumsy music of type-writer keys
And a wind-up gramophone
Mixing meaninglessly with voices from beneath
The unbearable window –
Its cold-blooded glass an impossible page
For amphibious nightmares
And free-falling verse.

Pushkin's Honeymoon House

A grey shadow gathered at the windows.
Faint the yellow walls,
Imagined floors where waning footsteps
Still tread from room
To echoed room.
Curtains held aside
To see the pale gold leaf
Of autumn poplars
Pressed against the heart.
Memory betrays the savage distance
From here to where his wife,
Countess Lanskaya, lies alone
Surrounded by the dead.

Swan Lake At The Mariinsky Theatre

On seats of pale turquoise velvet and gilt
We perch like clumsy birds
To see the metamorphoses
Of sinew and flesh and gravity
As something of swan,
The gawky feathered shift,
Heavy grace of laboured flight
Lifts us above the cliches
Of pirouette and poise.
So even a wrist
Silhouetted against painted rushes
Takes the curve of swan neck.

We are all web footed
Substance of escape,
Permitted to migrate
From the bony truths
Of cartilage and cold and death.

The Roof Tiles

Stacked in neat piles as though
waiting for Christopher Columbus
to return to the once-new world
and mend his roof;
terracotta tiles, snug against hand-made contours
each casting an arc of shadow
as though they know what the others
are thinking:
of paella and fingers against guitar strings in the night
of white pigeons and the rolling
Andalusian accent of the clouds
of dust and siesta and the surviving rhythms
of an old man asleep
of women at the birth,
of Holy Water sprinkled at the wake.

Not this savage sun,
this ruthless soil,
this easy, uneasy dying,
this pitiless, pitiless rain.

What The Spanish Brought

All that sea-borne terror,
manatees in dream,
warm flesh thoughts from the cold,
marinated fantasy;
wine and thirst and terracotta tiles,
ships and wood and impossible distance,
men and men and men and hunger,
blades of solid sunlight,
prayer and paleness,
dying and living and dying,
muscle and phlegm and fever and dry fear.

White Crosses

White crosses – when death doesn't ask your name.
White crosses – random markers of the rotting embrace between
                                                    flesh and soil.
White crosses – knowing that wherever we walk, we walk on graves.
Goose-bumps, rumours in the heat,
the spitting tremor of a spirit in our spine.
There among the flaming flamboyan,
the skin-pink grasses, cactus wall,
so far from old old worlds,
white crosses,
ghosts of misery, ankle-high.

AIDAN ROONEY-CÉSPEDES

BORN IN MONAGHAN IN 1965. HE LIVES IN MASSACHUSETTS WHERE HE HAS BEEN A TEACHER OF ENGLISH AND FRENCH AT THAYER ACADEMY FOR THE PAST FOURTEEN YEARS. IN 1996 HE WAS WINNER OF THE W.B. YEATS POETRY COMPETITION AND IN 1997 HE RECEIVED THE SUNDAY TRIBUNE / HENNESSY COGNAC AWARD FOR NEW IRISH POETRY. HIS FIRST COLLECTION OF POEMS 'DAY RELEASE' APPEARED FROM THE GALLERY PRESS IN 2000.

Lynx
Or poem beginning with half a line by Matthew Sweeney

Scrape the cat off the road, and continue on down
95, the hell out of Millinoket, Maine,
into the snow's hypnosis. Have your partner part
the winter fur on her thick neck, sedate the cat,
compose, for comfort, the great, lovely snow paws
and black rings of her short tail. Get a move on. Pause
once for a blast of drive-thru coffee, then beeline
it to Tufts. Call ahead. Say the job is feline.

Visit all spring. Comb the gray rime from her mane,
massage the buff underside. Once the screws have taken,
bear gifts of bird and fish, cutlets of venison,
endangered snowshoe hares. Rehab on a treadmill.
Come March, monitor for estrus. Show up with a male,
and watch, behind the mirror, wild cats make out mortal.

Francis Bacon And The Hen
Palais des Papes, Avignon

Men are alike in this:
whosoever gets
a good idea leaps,

as Bacon did, or
so the story goes,
out of the coach

to have a common hen
slain and gutted, raring
to stuff a ball of snow

in the hen's cavity, ice
as good a cure
as salt, and truth

an insufficient end.
He knows exactly
what he's about,

a hand in the bird,
what way Highgate is,
the price advancement

pays, and for three
listless, snowbound days
he drifts in and out,

feeling the nip of death.

The Visit

"e la domanda che tu lasci è anch'essa
un gesto tuo, all 'ombra delle croci" — Montale

Last night you were living with the neighbours.
They showed up with their boys as they always do,
on the porch some weekend evening, bearing a salad,
a bottle of red, a six-pack for themselves, and you

fell right in after them, no introductions, wearing
one of your flowered summer skirts and carrying
the big cream, ceramic bowl you started bread in.
Everyone smiled and kissed hello and acted normal

except for you, a certain coolness in your manner
as if to show some hurt that you hadn't been invited.
The seared tuna came out perfect on the new grill.
The kids behaved. I expected you to scold us

for the fuss, no call for half of it, the new kitchen
you escaped to while we sat down to food. "There's
a pretty little girl from Omagh in the County of Tyrone,"
I overheard you sing, and when you left with them

you left with me a wheaten loaf with the deep cross
you liked to score on top, your white fingers disappearing
to tell beads in your apron pocket, your lips lip-synching,
the core of the bread, underneath, in the middle, burning my palm.

The Name Takers
Palais des Papes, Avignon

The sun had been up and about its own
good measure of hours — no nap, no coffee-
break, no smoke, just the usual glances thrown
to the jaded youth in their latest, puffy
fashions, barely a nod to business
casuals out to lunch, dittoing this,
uploading that, no time for a Guinness
or a level chat, all *age quod agis* —

when the dead paraded through the streets.
It was more embarrassment than snafu,
really, that made people give up their seats,
the dead turning their noses up at tofu,
bagels, sashimi, before they ordered
bowl after bowl of potato *soupe du jour*,
spilling and slurping so much it bordered
on barbarism. You could tell they were poor

from their get up of boots and gaudy rags,
the men, though hewn, lean, rough-cut, big-handed,
the women mostly what we'd now call hags,
but if you weren't aware they'd just landed
in from Afterlife, you'd swear by the medley
of laughter and cracks, they were living proof
of the very well-off. Their irony was deadly,
their wit sharp, and after lunch they raised the roof,

literally, and hovered for a bit
like Peter Pans, before they lighted down.
They had come to see they didn't fit
in the busy streets of the modern town,
so they headed back the way they had come,

to their *status quo ante bellum*.
They belonged to no one. No one claimed them.
No chancers. No takers. No one said their name.

Survival

Stay put
if you can help it.
Always be ready to say kaput,-
but wear a helmet.
— Joseph Brodsky

Scant caveat for the double hairpin turn
our 2CV failed to quite negotiate,

that sigmoid a hundred yards back, squiggled
on an amber triangle behind a tree,

would echo the roadkill we ended up beside,
over-easy, driver's side, a few miles

far side of Falcarragh, were it not so far
along in its excited decomposition,

less the *bourdonnement* of bluebottles
than the cooperative wriggle of maggots

making heat in the bloated carcass someone'd
flung into long grass, roiling like a motor

at the heart of the badger, our own still ticking
over, one wheel spinning in mid-air, till

we tip it back on all fours and carry on,
the top rolled back, to the *Ostán* in Gweedore

for a swim and sweat, our pelts carving water
above our trawled shadows, then glistening side

by side on cedar bunks, aglow and pulsing
in the kind of heat that would make your breathing

something to think about if we hadn't talked,
then touched, putting all account behind us.

Why Muldoon

Why Muldoon took a crooklock across the head
landed him up in the County a bit concussed
was more a case of mistaken identity

(a bouncer up the Seasons came across him thrust

half-in half-out of the proprietor's ex-wife
's snazzy black leather interior Ford Capri,
and took him for one of the queogh-boy brothers F-,
panelbeaters down the Moy who, come Friday, would

hit a disco across the border for a car
for Saturday's sidejob breaking down her numbers)

than anything to get bent out of shape over,
although,
       between him and your man and the purr
           of motors ticking over,
               word got out there's no more
to it than the struck head Muldoon remembers.

MICHAEL S. BEGNAL

Born in 1966 and has been widely published in journals such as Poetry Ireland Review, Fortnight, College Green, The Stinging Fly, Comhar, Ropes, The Black Mountain Review, Poetry Scotland, Nerve, etc. His collection 'Ancestor Worship' (Salmon Poetry) is forthcoming.

Expatriation

Blue sky envelopes Galway
like the sea does Pádraigín
who drowned

American tourists sit
on the Claddagh bench
talking in Boston accents,
while a moth struggles uselessly
in the water
against its common death,
a kicking speck

like the oblivion of Boston,
cast from your gorted land
where rivers run free,
but not the minds
that aped their masters,
that aped their masters

and I too'm "American" now,
sauntering the local lanes,
this land of ghostly progenitors,
cold stone,
bitter defeat

Ancestor Worship

Not like the bones of parents
carried out in procession
from their dark vaginal tombs
among the rocks,
mummified skin stretched
and tanned in mockery of death

it's not like the imagined
rituals of an old old age
before iron or bronze,
the metal of our mythology,
though the faces look the same
in the rain

but the warm blood
that flows through to this age,
dangerous and violent in veins,
hanging heavy like burlap sheets
on a dewy day

the right hook of history,
the slow motion arc of the punch,
the strange figure
on a modern city street
who burrows into your eye
and says, "Who're you?"

It's like when Lennon laid
his *New York* album on you,
and appeared in pictures
in his new image—
Revolutionary,
sudden Irishman,
Manhattanite,

gritty…

like LeRoi Jones's move to Harlem,
broke with his white friends,
changed his name:

> ancestor worship
> is the only religion
> truly compatible
> with the fact
> of evolution

New Year's Day 1999

In the search for Hell's Kitchen
the wide Westside streets
lay hollow in the cold

to breathe,
    an assault:
each moment hard
as the metal face
of a 10th Ave. payphone

always the streets, of course,
always the streets,
as I sought a "street" culture,
the traces of its bitterness,
the green neon of its bars,
the canny underdog,
the White Negro,
the setting of antipodal rivalries,
compression

But the Westside streets lay hollow,
broken liquor bottle,
each year the same
solid pavement,
frozen streams of canine
    and primate
        piss

They all left because of money,
their slice of the hair pie,
full integration:
Lucky Charms for breakfast,
and shower with Irish Spring

I only turned east
(at an alien corner)
because of the temperature,
the Janus-month extremity
of the situation,
noted
another empty bottle,
Baileys in a doorway,
a brown paper bag,
warehouse,

        the monstrous ramp.

View From A Galway Window

Old World butcher shop
blue house
the rooftops
and smokestacks of crooked industry,
grey steeple
through the billowing steam
that blends into ugly
skies of repression
and clouds the window
like lace curtains

wires on rusted poles
tower above rickety man
(on his bike loaded down
with plastic bags full of lint)

the faint smell of sewage,
some girl ditches her dog
and a fat woman
heads for the beauty parlour,
open for Saturday business
this *Bealtaine*,
but all I see are
Mormon missionaries
sent severely from Utah

Seal Poem

I don't understand my dreams

Day spent watching seals in the river,
speckled heads bobbing through the surface,
curious faces peering over to the shore,
the built stone banks, the bridge,
and diving down again for fish,
dive-bombing seagulls plummeting
all around them

The cool thing is to make eye contact
with an inquisitive seal—
of course they have emotions,
curiosity is one—
and to give her a human name,
Speckle-head, or to get really serious
about it, *Breac-chinn*

At night I'm in a high-rise apartment building
with Jerry Seinfeld and some girls,
and someone pulled off his wig
revealing his blond crew-cut,
which just about ended everything

YVONNE CULLEN

BORN IN DUBLIN 1966. STUDIED LAW AND WAS CALLED TO THE BAR IN DUBLIN IN 1989, HAS NOT PRACTICED. WORKS FREELANCE AS A CREATIVE WRITING WORKSHOP FACILITATOR, AND, AS WELL AS POETRY, WRITE SCREENPLAYS, AND PLAY CELLO AND WRITE STRING ARRANGEMENTS FOR THE DUBLIN ALTERNATIVE ROCK BAND NORTHLIGHT RAZORBLADE. WAS THE 1997 WINNER OF LISTOWEL WRITERS' WEEK'S COLLECTION COMPETITION, AND HAVE WON NUMEROUS OTHER AWARDS FOR HER POEMS.

From the sequence: Invitation to the Air.

The books were usually little 'Almanachs'...they contained a mixture of religious and folk aphorisms, home remedies...potted histories, descriptions of famous trials and fairy tales. Earlier the Almanachs were called Grimoires...and contained both prayers and spells....
- Gillian Tyndall

The Way Anything Starts
I do not know what to say
about this kind of love
   Michael Ondaatje

The next second
never –
across the dark grass –
calling back to us:

 Years opening,

 hearing in music its
 ring's roped corners, for us,

 lines we'll be
 standing in our arms,

soon –
tall
as ourselves –
to dance with them
so long.

On The Way To Here
The next second never calling back towards us across the dark grass
 only the grass at our ankles –

on the way to here,
someone is crossing an opened marquee – thumb print
 of astonishment on a field behind a church
where I am, off a flight and trains, out of a lover's car
 minutes in hills in France, waiting out a phone call.

Black, under that church portal – and as deeply gold on windows:
 I stand hearing he and I won't be so happy.
The sky's frightening length again. And aloneness, there:
 like runways.

In the blue-green towards that tent
 The "Sorry!" and "Private!" we expect prepare their approaches.
Till you, behind a counter, smile, or send your clear look,

 contact that is sudden, water.

Garage doors wide, the bulk of your dog
 on the track, back thirteen kilometres.
In Paris, your boys' shining heads   Love:
something that "only starts well."
A year before I'll open a school report
 your eyes in its photograph
porous and tilted this same way   brother under the stars
 brother ahead of me.

Somebody sets up the bottles   We lift simple words
    laugh at ourselves passing them.

Sea Glass
Then someone writes a postcard
        to a hallway.
Odd words of it you carry,
        curves of sea glass.

Until, above a new start
        for a longer love
there's a name to a corner
        of the view.
A corner of sky white as
        paper is white
you could send it anything.

Until "My heart misses him,"
        is what you say
because you read a street's name
        you never used to notice.

At the open junction you
        want to stay with a man you love.

Is it down this his letter
plunges? Saying
"Time doesn't move any more."

Getting up in him in the
        morning
lying down in him at night,
        not answering.

Until: morning above your
        broken, patched up neighbourhood

"always thinking about him,"
    you said.

Your jacket on a chair –
    humble, desperate.

Until you stood in the rain
    you
could see pour to a garden.
    Had dropped to a madness,

Walked there, on the sinews in
    the air of a room.

This
Only after all this time
   This strange strong affection
Do I want words from behind clear ones
   This kind of love
From behind your first written hello
   Small bell over language
Want the thoughts – warm in the head – for someone
                               countries-far
   Lifting my face to the thought of you
Attempts to understand. Even doors in the mind turned
                                     back from

Crossing to the joy of it – where? – from that life: my keys
   ringing to the same table: this sweet, stark.

Your House
Here, mornings are the squeeze to the kitchen past the dog –
   to comedies of wreckage, doghair-clouded tiles.
From the window the cats force, day blows, round my dreams
   of learning to levitate, talking to my dead.

All night – cats, moths, stars on, and up the hill the road,
                                          the spring –
this window's invitation to the air,
  that - if I'd known it – would have frightened me.

Now Uncurl
Now uncurl
another evening's silence.

Towards the burn
of the docklights.

At the estuary
the streetlights' stars.

Wish it on: trawlers,
catamarans, rockfaces in it.

The pylons
down frozen England,

pubs,
drivers you'll never know.

The damp sand the sea the damp sand
in it.

For the moonshone tiles in his hall, it:
an arrow.

Not A Letter
The heart commands
The frost that gently captivates us....

                                            Paul Celan

Now I know enough
to see mid-morning.

Villages a white van leaps through.
A dream's speed has you in
clothes like yours –
from the wheel you turn towards me.
Strike of a match here, and a sentence from you flares.
Or I've thought one of your kids' names:
vivid, he's licking chocolate powder
from browned lips; shrugs…
the sheen and fall of his hair like laughter
is virtually here –
in a Camera Obscura where we could almost live,
an imagined river.

Here, the same
butterfly brings, five, six times to rest on a garden table
her wrought metal legs,
dips her wings to each absolute angle.
And presence means seeing it,
The heat of a forearm.
Now what I keep is settling,
some natural way –
like logs on your roadsides.
Into change, without nostalgia;
the blue past branches in an afternoon
become the end of
a life in which I mightn't see you.

Now I'd see for a long time,
at times, the stay of a life maybe
some clearer width of after rain in my days.
The sentences' cut sods
not disappointing us
nor that the letters would never be

gazettes from the routines
of shoelaces, dinners.

The silence we moved to would be never silence.
If midges in gardens
Rose, incandescent as laughs:
Often, breezes would travel one's table, the other's
                                                    windowsill.
What a small thing when we'd forget eachother,
Brother facing the blue facing the blackness.

The taps of the wings
uncountable,   over.

Kabuki
Your old words lean tips of flames towards me
                    sometimes. They
line walls, with the thoughts
                    of shadow lamps,
can be light: back like a level look from hills;
your meaning: joy. Joy:
what can be, with the man I love, here.

And someone will step forward
                    sometimes.
On a Sunday on T.V, the Kabuki actor say he will try
                    to dance love and mourning;
love – not physical, though that will be in it, and
                    the dubbed voices say for us: love
most like the love between a human
                    and a bird that rests near them

Small thing so true, it settles in my life –
                    on you, where you are, there,
we live it this lightly. And there's a night, when with…
            Franglais, and Ancais

    we fix human importance
               (alongside dead flies)
resolve the world (even Bach) to one of those "things like an
               upside-down glass"
whose domed shape loved hands would make,
               whose snow they would have fall
with loved fingers, so I'd peel a life from myself
               to accompany the life you'd have,
I'd reach it out – my shy hand on your head –
               believe you keep it.

All it Was

That country, with its after-rain
rising, like us with language: all we'd say.
The drying rain that stands up out of roadsides
in its own time…floats to a windscreen.

That can come to me anywhere;
when wet greens, shredded on a board, brought me to it:
the bend for Fayot.

One day when I said
to the us among whitenesses: as long as,
longer than you'd live, I'd think warmly of you.

In my kitchen, that mist – become ones
who never got to return. Back
for their allowed hour
between their fields and their loved forests.

The drying rain, that, in such country,
stands, out of roadsides, triangled lengths –
the same, never precisely; that
– each in its own time – swims to the windscreen,

becomes this haunting,
this grazing flying.

TOM FRENCH

BORN IN 1966, HIS FIRST COLLECTION 'TOUCHING THE BONES' WAS PUBLISHED BY GALLERY PRESS IN 2001 AND HAS BEEN SHORT-LISTED FOR A FORWARD PRIZE. HE LIVES IN DUBLIN WITH HIS WIFE AND SON.

Estate

Sharp TV, mantle clock, (black, no pendulum),
spark guard, china, box of jewelry (costume);

Ten paperbacks including Casement's *1916*,
nest of tables, brass log box, Dresden figurine;

Light fittings, bedside lamps, Deca exercise bike,
eight oils on board (signed), titled *Lamb of Christ*.

Two Verbs For 'To Be'

When trying to decide when to use which
the books will be of no help whatsoever
because you haven't grown up in the language.

The first is used to speak of permanent states –
time, possession, origin, inherent characteristics.
It is five o'clock. The watch is gold. We're English.
It is better to wait though it is difficult to learn.

The second will cover all temporary states –
The children are playing in the garden.
Carmen is upstairs. The train is about to leave.

These basic rules will not cover every situation.
There are cases where it is difficult to decide.
For the verbs 'to be young' and 'to be rich'
use the first. For 'to be in love' use the second.

Only experience will teach you the difference.
She is Italian. The apples are in the kitchen.
The house is on the hill. It is dangerous to smoke.
The children are upstairs asleep. Now translate.

Blood

She returns the Visa you gave her in error,
takes your hand and pricks your little finger.
By the time the drop of your blood she releases
hits rocks bottom you know her from somewhere,
so you take the plunge and ask her to supper
in a cybercaf on the outskirts where the waitress
palms what you slip her for a booth in the corner.
When the cashier swipes it the machine accepts
Your blood donor card, though you're in the red.
And a couple of bottles of the house plonk later
her uniform is draped on the back of a chair
and she's kissed the vein in your forearm better.
The tiny silver pelican that comes weeks later
draws a dark red pearl from the identical finger.

Listening Test

Madame Madeleine Garin will be recalling
her feelings on the morning scores of tanks
arrived at the hamlet where she was living
with her family in the 30s in Haute Provence.

The material will be played through 3 times;
first, at the normal speed of a news bulletin;
then in segments with pauses, then through again,
the same procedure as for people taking German.

Try to establish, as soon as you can, the number
of siblings she mentions and where she comes,
the day of the week and the time of day, (remember
the words I gave you for 'twilight'. She uses one).

The question relating to the number of eggs
 her mother's sister brings, and the final one
about injuries sustained to her spine and legs
are minor by comparison with the 2-part one –

why Madeleine could be considered (i) fortunate,
(which, for higher level people, is the crucial one),
and (ii) in another way, unfortunate?
Though you will, undoubtedly, be hearing things

you mightn't've heard in English before, stay calm.
All you will need is a clean sheet of paper and a pen.
If no one has any questions we may as well begin.
The next person you will hear will be Madame Garin.

Saint Anthony Preachng To The Fish

Flush with the rough dash of this fishing lodge porch
it amounts to no more than the tile it is, depicting
Anthony standing at the bank of rippling water, crimpled
into tiny waves, swimming in his huge Franciscan habit,
transfixing the assembled masses with his pinprick eyes.
And they are ranged before him in the river, good as gold –
sharks at the back, sea horses and barracudas, bright pupils
jostling to be near their teacher, attentive salmon soaking up
the lecture, lifting their bodies to hear him clear of the water.
I'd love to be able to eavesdrop on him, this nervous mystic

practicing his rhetoric on fish to be word perfect when he goes
before the people. Does he send them back to the riverbed
to love and serve their maker the way our curate on Sunday did?
And do the young sprat burst out crying when he thumps the air,
indicating heaven and accusing them of being *Ye of little faith!*,
terminating the sermon, sending water dwellers diving down
for cover. (His raised hand hints he is chastising them for some
                                       excess of joy in being fish).
But the version I prefer's the other tile –
Anthony still by the river, this time stripped, like those youngsters
on the railway bridge at Ardnacrusha in the height of summer.

He has slipped his head through the neck-hole in his habit
Like the eye of a needle or a loop-hole in scripture, pressed
The flats of his hands together as if in rapture, arched in the air
And jack-knifed, splitting the skin of the river with a brilliant dive;
Or bombed, his thin arms wrapped around his knees, leaving
The ceramic empty for eternity of everything except the habit
On the riverbank, empty of Anthony, and the congregation baffled,
Gaping skyward and at each other, wondering did they dream it
And would the annals have it, that the saint resurfaced, spurted
Like a fountain and told them all the show was over,
                                            to just go home.

'Nationalism In Music' (1982)
i.m. James French (1965-1987)

The only surviving recording of your voice
is the school music project on a tape cassette
they shipped home with your personal effects.
My ghost cognoscente, my musical enthusiast,
I wanted to ask what difference music makes,
rewinding it for months to hear you pronounce
'*N-a-a-a-tionalism*', and '*nineteen-tirty-tree*',
the great names '*Borodin, Smetana, Mussorgsky.*'
I think I should have seen you in your cask,
touched your broken legs, your smashed wrists
rested my palms against the bruise of your face.
When I play it now I play it to hear, more
than anything else, *'the music that springs*
                      directly from the earth, from

JAMES McCABE

BORN IN DUBLIN IN 1966. EDUCATED AT UNIVERSITY COLLEGE DUBLIN AND HOLDS A PhD FROM OXFORD UNIVERSITY, FOR WHICH HE WAS AWARDED THE BRITISH COUNCIL MILLENNIUM SCHOLARSHIP. HIS FIRST COLLECTION 'THE WHITE BATTLEFIELD OF SILENCE' BEING PUBLISHED IN 1999. HE WON THE SCOTTISH INTERNATIONAL POETRY PRIZE IN 1998, AND IS ALSO THE WINNER OF TWO HAWTHORNDEN FELLOWSHIPS. AT PRESENT WORKING ON A SECOND COLLECTION, 'SCENES FROM THE AFTERLIFE'.

Eagle's Nest

Our little corporal has left Olympus,
The island Alp above the world, and gone
Underground the god, at least, of his own
Bunker, berserk in the shirt of Nessus.

His world shrinks in the magnifying glass
Who held the future with an eagle's eye,
And dreams again the wet trench, the greasy
Backstreet, lost in a cloud of coloured gas . . .

In the window it was always summer,
The sugarbowl snow, the silver tray lake.
Tyrants in the afternoon almost took
Leave of their senses, ate cake, took pictures.

But this is more recent: Berchtesgaden
Broken under a blue sky, blank ashes,
And absent the hosts of such emptiness –
Adolf, Eva, burning in the garden.

April 1945

Clare Island Revisited

Heading west, the road curls up to where trees
Branch out and embrace themselves, until whale
Shapes at last float out through the ancient mist:
Clew Bay, all Tír na nÒg in smithereens.

Heading west, the boat rolls in a slate grey
Sea until the mainland is lost in thought
And the island comes close like a live dream,
Cut like a key to complete the jigsaw.

Heading west, the road turns to grass until
Nothing but pure cliff and sheer sky is left.
Lazybed ribs are the bones of a poem
Where famine lost its voice and became ghost.

Your crooked teeth tore Armada's belly
And swallowed *El Gran Grin* like a stone, then
You closed your lips on the foreign tongue, *brón
Na dtonnta as seo amach agus riamh.* ⋆

⋆ *Sadness of the waves from now on and before.*

An Angel Surveys The Ruins Of Dresden

In your hand you seem to hold
All the rubble of Europe,
As if you had waited for
This one chance to come alive,
Or offer something maybe
To the skeleton city
By way of flesh or nurture.

From the City Hall you watched
The labyrinth fill with flame,
But could not move your black robes
Or turn your face away from
The indescribable rose
That gathered all its fury
On the dark stem of the Elbe.

They are burning the dead, heaped
Like leaves, unidentified,
Who dreamt about the future
As if the war were over,
Before the black bombers came
And pulled a blanket of flame
Across the sleeping city.

Dresden angel, how could you know
When the sirens screamed all clear
That this was not the end ?
That more would share your salt tears
In the terrible desert,
Your stone and frozen sorrow,
Mar aingil gan Dia . . . ★

★ *Like angels without a God . . .*

Soundings
In Memoriam Augustine Martin

The little battalions march out
Onto the white battlefield of silence.
Poetry, you said, was like an empire
Surrounded by barbarians, monsters
In the margin. For years like legionnaires
We fought along its cold northern borders.
October like a funeral of leaves
Took you on its shield, our dead emperor,
The wind blowing through our heavy armour,
And the horses of sound on a white field.

Oradour Sur Glane

On Saturday 10th June 1944, the village of Oradour-Sur-Glane in France was surrounded by soldiers of the Waffen-SS. Over six hundred inhabitants were massacred and the village left a burning wreck. No definite cause for the action has ever been found.

And then one afternoon late in the war
History arrived in trucks. Instead of
First holy Communion the schoolchildren
Taken out and promised sweets, photographs.
Instead of shopping and the tobacco
Ration, the village suddenly strange with
The foreign voices and the camouflage.
Instead of the afterdinner coffee
Hotel guests told to assemble quickly
Outside with the others – covered with flour,
The baker stripped to the waist; the half-shaved;
The sick schoolteacher in her dressing gown;
The friend on a visit, unable to
Trust the calm assurance of the mayor,
Not knowing the novelty of terror
One Saturday afternoon in summer.
Again and again in his copybook
A boy had written out in punishment
The sentence: *Je prends la resolution*
De ne jamais faire de mal aux autres.

Unburied, the warm ochre of your bones
Grows long shadows in the late evening sun.
Altar and bath are open to the sky,
The doctor's car a holocaust of rust
And birds alone to watch the falling leaf.
Still the river is a mirror for its

Trees as they replace the leaves of each year,
But here in this archaeology of
Empty streets the tramlines and telegraph
Poles are waiting for Godot. Here silence
Is a souvenir, a sewing-machine
Left on a window sill until nothing
But pure idea of things is left:
The penknife and the watch, the wedding ring,
The cigarette case punctured with a hole,
The extinct clock that stopped, and then started
Counting the minutes of eternity,
The pale flush of leaves in a summer breeze,
The slow snow falling from a blindfold sky,
De ne jamais faire de mal aux autres.

One by one and years later the guilty
Die, surrounded by friends and family,
From natural causes. Unless they too
Were slaughtered in the aftermath – battle
Massacre where no coward could find hope.
But for the one who lived it merely meant
Getting on with things, forgetting the war,
The black and white photographs, moving back
Into the colour film of his real life.
Except, possibly, once in a while when
A dream sweats him awake, back there again:
'Today you're going to see the blood flow.'
Six hundred in a single afternoon,
And not a loss to show for it, but for
The single accidental casualty,
Dropping down dead under a falling brick.
They too were human after all, given
The last, tragic irony – some of them
Alsatian and Frenchmen like yourselves,
De ne jamais faire de mal aux autres.

The faces smile in the photographs that
Tell each grave apart, children looking to
The future, all innocence unconscious,
Out of the unimaginable past:
Of bicycles along green summer lanes,
Of polka dot trout flashing in the Glane,
Of birthdays, the fluttering butterfly,
The tram's familiar, friendly hum before
The caterpillar squeal of a halftrack.
The rest unidentified, buried as
One flesh, except for two glass coffins where
The charred, indiscriminate bones of some
Offer themselves for display; other ones
Discovered at the bottom of a well,
Or shot escaping halfway through a fence,
The infant found in the baker's oven,
The old man left for dead in his own blood,
Or hurriedly buried in shallow graves,
One blind hand reaching up through the garden,
De ne jamais faire de mal aux autres.

In the church the women and children wait,
As their men are led into garages
And barns. No one knows how long it will take,
The officer pauses for translation,
Something about terrorists, that was it,
One afternoon at a quarter past two,
The war at an end, the ordeal over,
Clouds clearing after the morning drizzle.
At half past three the church bell, then stutter
Of a machine gun as the killing starts,
The furious agreement of small arms
Before the last, diligent pistol shots,
The crackle of sparks, the dark cloud, the sound
Of a German voice on the gramophone.
Days later at the burnt-out church a man

Comes across his wife holding her mother,
Both bodies at a touch disintegrate,
The little churchbells melted in the heat,
The bullet-riddled pram at the altar,
De ne jamais faire de mal aux autres.

Nevermore to harm others, a promise
That was easily kept. Now clouds like ghosts
Through the summer move, and all possible
Harm cannot again disturb the sudden
Permanence of this place. Oradour, lost
Ocean inside the shell, the syllables
Of your name can never translate into
The beautiful excuse of poetry,
But only an empty hush of leaves where
Tramtracks rust in the cobblestone silence,
Suddenly ancient as Thira or lost
Atlantis, swallowed in the avalanche.
The fire-black bicycle hangs on a wall,
Unused to such capricious idleness,
And wooden shutters shipwreck in the sun.
In a dream's aerial photography
I flew over your honeycomb ruin,
Village of a thousand whispers, from which
History now has departed for good,
Leaving you with all the time in the world.

NIALL McGRATH

Born 1966 in Antrim and is a graduate of the Ulster and Edinburgh Universities. His publications include a novel, 'Heart of a Heartless World' (1995); poetry pamphlets, 'First Sight' (1997) 'Déjà vu' (1999) and 'First World' (2002); and the translitertations, 'Godsong & A Matter Of Honour' (2000). He has won several poetry prizes. He is editor of The Black Mountain Review and widely published as a reviewer.

Moon Calf
(Black Mountain, Belfast, Winter)

Missed when the three brothers took the herd off the hill
At the back end of the year, he tripped about
Up there on the heathery slopes till the snow came;
Braved drifts alone, pawing through freezing sheets
To nibble at icy tufts; sheltered in gullies from
March rains that poked his ribs like cold-steel rods;
Shied away from the scraps of lunchtime pieces
The transmission station men tossed over the fence at him.

Come the late spring, you'd see his sleek form fill out,
His charolais coat redden as the primroses budded;
April nights he'd defy the last chilly gusts to stand
On the summit, silhouetted against the moon's clarity;
How his head bobbed high when the lorry tail dropped
And the new cows and calves skittered into his company.

Aurora Borealis
(Jan 1972)

Grieve for the child in his pyjamas
Shivering in the cool of a Sunday night
As he stands wide-eyed and incredulous
Staring out through the front door's glass panel
As if it were a TV. For on the screen
Of the horizon what amazes
Him is the spectacle of Northern Lights –
Roman Legionnaires on the march across
The Ulster skyline, implanting a spell
In his young mind, which will cause him to yearn
To recapture wild excitement now felt.
Grieve for the child: this display does not scare
Him; he adores, revels in, his senses melt,
Suffuse with blood-red glory in the air.

In The Piggery

The pighouse was warm on winter evenings;
An infra-red lamp glowed in the corner
Of the pen, where our sow and her weaners
Languished. Smell of dust. Sound of their sucklings.

I used to love cradling those delicate
Piglets, sensing their soft, pink wriggling shapes;
Amused by tottering, innocent japes
I'd watch their wet snouts nuzzle for a teat.

The pale ears were paper-thin, veined, would wilt
At my touch; black, beady eyes glared wildly
When I'd lift them, trotters kicking madly
Like the heart thud-thudding within each chest.

But every litter seemed to have a runt.
It became expected of me to raise
Skeletal, lukewarm ones with their blank gaze,
Against the wall give their skulls a swift dunt.

So the sty ceased to be an oasis
From weary farmyard bustle or cold wind,
Became a place where betrayed faces grinned.
A light doesn't just heat, sometimes it scorches.

from Njal's Saga, Section 157

Flosi offered to go with Earl Sigurd
On his Irish expedition, but was refused –
Flosi still had to carry out his pilgrimage
To Rome as part of his settlement. The stage
Was set for a spectacular confrontation,
Even if Flosi was not going to be one
Of the participants. When Sigurd reached
Dublin on Palm Sunday, Brodir had already beseeched
Black spirits by means of sorcery what way
The battle would go. He learned that if the day
Of conflict was Good Friday, Brian Boru
Would win the fight but lose his life; Brodir knew,
Also, that if the battle occurred before
Friday, Brian's foes would be cut down like wildflowers
In a cornfield. Brodir said they should not engage
The Irish before Friday. On the Thursday
A man came on a dapple-grey horse to parley
With Brodir and Kormlod before the carnage.
Brian did not want to field arms on Good Friday,
So a wall of shields was formed around the King
As the two armies, bright in their battle array,
Lined up face-to-face, each side's banners flanking
Their leaders. When the clash commenced, Brodir
Waded through the enemy ranks without fear.
Meeting Ulf Hreda, Brodir was knocked down
Three times, each time struggling to his feet again;
But at last he fled into the forest.
Earl Sigurd's standard-bearer was butchered,
So he ordered Thorstein Hallsson to hoist
The standard; he was about to do so when he was told
Those who carried it would all end up dead.
Annoyed, Earl Sigurd ordered Hrafn the Red

To carry the standard. "Carry your own
Devil yourself!" Hrafn snapped. The earl ripped the worn
Flag from its staff and tucked it inside his armour,
Saying, "A beggar should carry his own bundle."
Shortly after that, Sigurd was killed by a spear.
Ospak was severely wounded and terrible
Gashes claimed the lives of both Brian's sons.
Despite this, Sigtrygg's men were routed and ran.
Doing so, Thorstein Hallsson had to stop to tie
His shoe-thong. Kerthjalfad,
Seeing Thorstein's
Lack of urgency, said, "Do you want to die?
Why're you loafing here?"
                              "Why should I burst my spleen?
I won't reach home tonight. I'm from Iceland."
He was spared by the chortling Kerthjalfad.
Hrafn the Red was chased into a strong river.
He prayed, "Your dog has run twice to Rome, Saint Peter,
And would do so a third time if you allowed it."
He was freed by the devils in the current.
Brodir saw that Brian's men were harassing
Fugitives and only a few manned the King's
Wall of shields. He darted from the forest
And hacked at Brian. Young Todk tried to protect
His master with an arm, but both it and Brian's
Head were cut off. It is rumoured when the man's
Blood spilled over the boy's stump the wound healed
Rapidly. Brodir had the word spread round
That the Irish King was dead. Brian's officers,
Surrounding Brodir and his men, smothered their spears,
Axes and swords with tree branches and took
Them prisoner. Brodir had his belly
Slit open and intestines wound round an oak
So that he died slowly and miserably.
All Brodir's men were put to the sword, too.
Brian's body was laid out; the head seemed grafted to

His neck again. Fifteen of the Burners of Njal
In this Battle of Clontarf were despatched to Hell.
That same morning, in Caithness, a man, Dorrud,
Had seen twelve riders approach a woman's crude
Cottage and go inside. When Dorrud had peered
Through a window he had seen the women, heads bowed,
Around a loom. Men's heads were in place of weights;
Intestines were being used as warp and weft;
A sword served as beater; the shuttle was an arrow.
The women were chanting an eerie anthem
As they operated the loom between them:
"The Valkyries are weaving with swords, now,
Spear-shafts will shatter and shields will splinter
As axes gnash like wolves fangs through armour.
Lands will be ruled by new peoples who once lived
In obscurity in outlying headlands.
Erin will suffer a grief that'll never fail
To sting the eyes or ache the hearts of Cruthin and Gael.
The web is now woven,
The battlefield reddens;
News of grave disaster
Spreads through provinces four.
Let them who listen to our Valkyrie song
Take it to heart and pass it on to their throng;
Let's ride our horses hard, bareback – with no fear,
But rather, with swords unsheathed – away from here."
They tore the cloth from the loom and ripped it apart;
Then, the twelve mounted their horses to depart.
In the Faroes, Brand Gneistason saw the same
Fantastic display. In Iceland, the hem
Of a priest's stole became spotted with blood
As if by magic, so much blood it soaked
Him to the skin; at another place a priest
Saw an ocean beside the altar, full of sea-beasts.
In Orkney, Harek thought he saw Earl Sigurd
And rode across the plain to meet his friend

And lord; they were seen to meet and ride behind
A hill, but no trace of Harek was ever found.
In the Hebrides, Earl Gilli dreamt a man
Called Herfid came to him, saying he had just been
In Ireland. Herfid told the earl that Sigurd
Had been killed, as had Brian – but Brian had conquered.
Flosi, who was staying at Earl Gilli's court,
Kept discussing his vision with him till a report
Arrived from Ireland – Hrafn the Red made it home.
He told them all the Vikings and all Flosi's men
Were killed, except his brother-in-law, Thorstein.
Flosi told Earl Gilli he would now head for Rome.
The earl gave Flosi a ship, supplies and silver;
And so he launched off in a longboat once more.

JOSEPH WOODS

BORN IN 1966 AND TRAINED AS A SCIENTIST, HE TRAVELLED EXTENSIVELY IN ASIA AND JAPAN. HE HOLDS AN MA IN CREATIVE WRITING (LANCASTER UNIVERSITY) FROM POETS' HOUSE. HE HAS BEEN WIDELY PUBLISHED IN JOURNALS BOTH HOME AND ABROAD AND IS CURRENTLY DIRECTOR OF POETRY IRELAND. HIS COLLECTION 'SAILING TO HOKKAIDO' WAS PUBLISHED IN 2001 BY WORPLE PRESS.

Sicilian Sketches

...many times I have lost myself in the sea.
Unaware of the water, I go searching a death
in which light consumes me.
Gacela de la Huida, Garcia Lorca

1. Rain

Yesterday's rain of rice on the steps
of the Basilica di San Sebastiano
is rained upon by today's drizzle.

Kernels hold firm against a wind
that will not scatter what the hand has.
Vows are now a day old

and celebrations cease to the clang
of colossal bronze doors,
a sound seal on memory.

Beyond the balustrade, a mere mizzle
has flushed streets clean of activity,
licked the lava pavements and painted

colour on the faces of stone statues.
In the corner of a ricefield in Asia,
a farmer and his wife make love

while seed-shoots are sown
into a waiting earth. I did not see
anything and if I was there,
I was only sleeping.

2. Instructions
Perch yourself on the rocks and prepare
(the good eye on the Ionian)

for the wave to wash over and feed you in.
Take to the swell and aim for the horizon.

Ignore the undertow and slow lung-lapping
then sudden failure to float as a dead man.

Fall into the green, the green arms
of anaesthesia, you are more water now than ever.

3. Flotsam
Hours in a hospital bed where nothing
matters, only the benign
feed of a drip into the left arm.

The indignity of putting people out
and being back again. Whispering
glances at this daft, naked and hirsute

foreigner who took to our waters
and swam out on his own
having no need of Sirens.

My wet lungs for a cigarette,
only hours before the earthly
addictions assail again.

Saved, saved by the grip
of a stranger, the drag ashore
to a voice in the ear that insisted.

How many parts of one drown...
my mother's sister, was she four or five?
A nearly evaporated swallow-hole,

still a Pacific for a four year old:
her father's abandoned herding,
her brown hair, yellow summer dress.

I did not hear anything
and if I was there I was sleeping.

4. Dream
I stand on coarse sand to see
where things meet
my gnarled hands
liquid feet.

5. Villa Palagonia
We pass through a cordon grotesque
and into the villa Palagonia,
where each gargoyle
was commissioned by the Count
to drive his wife insane.

Our steps echo on tiles
of an empty ballroom where
mirrors on ceilings once
distorted dancers into monsters.
They have tarnished now to gunmetal

and hardly reflect light. Open shutters
on noon frame a stone demon, leaping

over a wall for two centuries. Three
of us here and the thought of a waltz

dissipates in the heat, fades
like the frescoes of bad taste.
A cat that's strayed inside
stops to lick its paws.

6. Passeggiata
In this immensity my thought is drowned:
And shipwreck sweet for me within this sea.
　from The Infinite, Leopardi

From the balcony, distant peaks darken
to oriental as evening passes. A square
beneath fills as it has done for centuries,
leaving the countryside to darkness and itself.
The toll of being outside walls still haunts,
only the odd or brave live there.
Now young and old begin the *passeggiata*
circulating through streets into a piazza
and back again; the vascular system
of every southern town. I sip a see-through
wine harvested from the plains below,
my kidneys still sore and sour with salt.
Here, with hardly a notion, I could begin again.
Knowing the heart and some of its arteries.

7. At Cefalu Cathedral
Roger II sailing from Salerno to Reggio in 1131 got caught in a storm and
fearing he would drown, vowed to build a cathedral if he survived.
He landed at Cefalu.

Churches the world over,
possessed by the same scent-

cruets laid on a local lace,
one half-empty, sticky and sanguine.

Christ looks down from the apse,
from gold heights, severe

and Norman as the glint of a blue
eye on this island. His book opened

at the words,
light of the word.

And an Arabic air to this nave, no light
lozenges fall on these flags

-more a glow, while Palermo still looks
east at siesta. The right hand gestures

a Bodhisattva silence, inscrutable
Norman in a mid-day Byzantine gloom.

8. Ice
Perhaps it was an iceberg
That he had glanced at on his journey from Japan.
     from Lough Derg, Patrick Kavanagh

Brought up to believe
that even walking near water
was enough to draw you in,

the stagnant canal and that pram
rusting among the miasma. Waves too,
in the numerous sea, always away

and never toward any openings.
Then, that journey north where

Japan, ceasing to look like itself,

turned its frontier face
to the frozen sea of Okhotsk.
And on arrival the ice had cracked,
a thaw of yellow slabs creaked
and groaned under the enormous
weight of the break up.

There was nothing to do having
reached it, except stroll on
the grey shore and consider

the journey back. My mother's father,
was seventy odd, when he saw the sea
for the first time and remarked to her

in his soft midlands mantra,
Such a lot of water…
an awful lot of water.

Mrs. Moon

Vibrato of cicada and crackle of a wood fire behind us,
me and the old man sitting on the stoop, chewing betel
to pulp and spitting out its blood. We gaze down
on the darkening valley, peaks rise before us and rice
terraces in their thousands. One hundred and fifty
something on one slope before I stopped counting,

lost in wonder, darkness, and then just losing track
with those walls of stone, drawn a score of centuries ago.
A scaffold or web as if holding the weight of a mountain;
strange how things settle, to take on weight like that.
Like stairs now or steps to the heavens, ascending peaks
that shift, reveal themselves between mists and cloud

of a microclimate. *Here comes Mrs. Moon* again…
says the old man spitting crimson and turning down
a cigarette …when *Mr. Cloud has gone.* The black
of the highest appears as if disembodied, we thought
we were high and there it is, lost in the negative space
of some vast woodblock print. Moonlight files a glint

over water held in an ancient field. Laughter comes
from the kitchen, old man's wife and you. We've come
through, we've come through. Tomorrow, Christmas Eve,
we'll head down the valley, you and I, and there being no paths
we'll walk the walls, lured by the sound of falling water,
to bathe in the bottomless blue they talk about.

Cagayan de Oro

All night the ship listed and rolled in the swell,
its engines cranking and grinding, keeping us awake,
alert and nervous after upgrading to first class. No
different from tourist class, except for a damp room
and our own portion of deck, but better by a long shot
than economy; leaving you exposed on the lower deck,
the heat of the engines, night, and the air thick
with the crying of children and mosquitoes.

The thought of seven thousand islands and as many
ferries got me through the night, our ship while old
and rusting was once Japanese. Morning then,
and being alive seems more secure in daylight,
we took our instant coffee within sight of land.
A pair of dolphins criss-crossed the prow
and thought better, before departing. Decks filled
and I saw boys dive into the harbour,

surprised they were heading for us, so far out.
Swarming as the ship stalled to point itself right,
darker than the brown they were swimming in.
We looked down from three storeys to their beckoning
as silver flashed in the sun and the scramble for it,
as they dived in the three-second life silver has
from surface to murk. A boy would emerge, placing
one peso in the purse of his mouth.

The brown five-peso coin had no life here, so silver
kept streaming until the throwers grew bored, casting
obliquely to make them work for it, swim the distance
and perhaps miss the plumb fall of the peso. Like throwing
crumbs at carp and watching the mill, it amused, no rope
having gone out yet. A coin aimed accidentally I think, disappeared

near the propeller's churn, then passengers became distracted
with disembarking. Boys struggled ashore with gobs swollen,

one hundred counted for our coffee. One boy rested
on the thick rope that was tying us to Cagayan de Oro.
In local language *cagayan* means shame.
The Spanish struck gold here.

DEIRDRE CARTMILL

BORN IN MOY, CO TYRONE IN 1967. HER POETRY HAS BEEN PUBLISHED WIDELY IN MAGAZINES AND JOURNALS. SHE WAS SHORTLISTED FOR A HENNESSY AWARD IN 1999 AND HAS BEEN A FINALIST IN THE SCOTTISH INTERNATIONAL OPEN POETRY COMPETITION. IN 2000 SHE RECEIVED AN AWARD FROM THE ARTS COUNCIL OF NORTHERN IRELAND. SHE FEATURED IN POETRY IRELAND'S INTRODUCTIONS SERIES IN 1999. HER FIRST COLLECTION IS DUE FOR PUBLICATION IN 2004. SHE LIVES IN BELFAST.

Aftermath

My dad spent the day ferrying the dead to the barrack's makeshift
                                                                                               morgue.
His bloodstained nails fleshed out the truth behind the first tense
                                                                                               headlines.

In a daze, he decommissioned his paramedic uniform,
dumped jacket, shirt, socks, trousers, even his shoes in our kitchen bin.

He smashed the lid down hard, lashed out until the tears crashed over
the no-man's-land of his eyes. Powerless, I watched him surrender to
                                                                                           his cries.

I'd spent that day firing words at a blank page, trying to breathe life
into their dead weight. I surveyed my cache of notebooks, suddenly
                                                                                                aware

my vision was useless to this man who gave life back to the dying.

Night Watch

I rub our kitten's back, the length of her tail
as if I'm fingering worry beads;

she curls on my knee, one eye open,
defying sleep,

sucks on my finger like a teat
then licks my hand clean, as if

it's I who rely on her.
When she stretches out and opens up

her white belly
wanting to be tickled and stroked

her innocent trust frightens me.

At night I creep out
and bend my ear to her conch-like mouth,

I rest my hand on her fur,
feel the rise and fall of each fragile breath,

counting down each heartbeat
until she wakes in the morning

and paws the hanging mobiles,
stilled and silent

since the last unwitnessed breath
of our first baby.

Drive By

We heard five pistol cracks
followed the flashing blues to the top of the street
where his blood was splayed like a blasted poppy on the tarmac.
A paramedic blessed himself at his feet
then covered his body with a yellow blanket
and there he lay, exhibit
A, until they wrapped him in a white forensic tent.

Behind their cordons they will comb
for bullets, blood, boot prints, tyre tracks,
their helicopters will hover low over the bungalows,
they will set up checkpoints and ask
the right questions but they won't stop
the siren wails, the dawn door knock
following the next fatal shot.

Long Home

1. White Petals

They had to shave the sides to ease you in
slicing the soil with a shovel. Three times
they dunked the coffin, hauled it back. Each time
I steadied myself for the moment when
You'd sink out of sight and I'd leer
into that hole to throw a single red rose
into the muck. But you just wouldn't go.
Sweet Jesus, dear god, let it be over.
The river dredges up the abbatoir's
debris and the stench makes me retch
as I scatter white petals from the Little Flower's
touring relics over your wilting wreaths.
As you lie facing the chapel do you pray
for me who has no words to heal this day?

2. Plot

Mum scooped a handful of marble stones
from the Republican plot to steady
the vase on your grave and I imagined you turning,
a man of peace lying under the green.
You were of a time when Ulster was shocked
by the murder of a judge's daughter,
yet you stared down death every day. The love notes
say you shouldered strangers stories and tears.
How did it feel when your world turned,
forced to beg for a job and a home,
becoming a suspect, a target, interned
in an ambulance uniform. You could have lifted a gun
but you chose to lift massbooks and stretchers.
Could you have chosen different if you weren't our father?

3. Mission Cross

I am a gravedigger stealing your last moments,
ransacking my memories to write these poems
but of what should I write? The apple blossoms falling
like shed skin, the pansies planted on newly turned soil,
the crucifix nailed behind glass doors,
the wounds of Jesus hidden by the sun's reflections?
I am obsessed with how you reached this place,
weeks watching your body fold and fade.
Now you lie like peat in the old priest's garden
where you used to grow spuds, turnips
and tomatoes under polythene, a miracle
in this cold climate – your only miracle.
You linger, the words of faith hewn
on the Mission Cross, 'ever old, ever new'.

Monolithic Venus

We have come to bury our dead by the twelve standing stones
at the top of Slieve Croob. The sun's flame
is snuffed by the ice slopes as we struggle uphill.

We step over a trickle seeping from an underground stream
– a trickle that flexes its infant muscles
until it surges into Belfast as the Lagan's dead weight pull.

Each upward curve reveals a new sight – the Mournes rising
as if erupting for the first time, a forest of aerials, masts and satellite dishes
taking root in the brown earth and sponge-soft green fern.

We climb over a toothless barbed wire fence
take shelter in the one surviving cairn,
a stone ark crowning the mountain.

Like a ballerina on a music box, I stand and slowly circle from the
                                                                                               seawashed
pastel painted houses at Newcastle, up the rough-cut coastline
over Spa Lough to Belfast, where Napoleon's nose snubs the city.

My eyes dance on, across Cavehill and the Black Mountain
beyond Lisburn and the pit of Lough Neagh, to the tangle
of murder triangle towns, trying to pick out the one I grew up in.

The car clogged arteries bleed into the Mournes and I come full circle
to the contours of your face, the paths I've travelled suddenly erased,
a stranger in what had once been my homeland.

Slumped down in our stone grave, you pass me a tea stained cup
construct your juju of milky tea, while I place another rock on the cairn,
a superstitious stepping stone to something.

Darkness beats time with our descent; before the sun blinks off
the crescent moon holds up the first star
and I wonder if you make a wish as we slip between day and night.

We sink into the ice speckled mud; I offer you one of my gloves,
too small and narrow for your male hand but you force and fist
your way into its warmth, until we each lope lopsided

with one hand surrendering to the night, the other
clenched in a pocket, our feet sucked down
as we look to the stars and curse their broken promises.

Karaoke In The Glasshouse

The ritual begins on my knees on the cold tiles,
the slow in and out, retching in darkness.
I flush the stains, flee to my local
a glass fronted victim of the new Belfast
where mosaic shopfronts no longer shatter
in a starshower of razor edged reflections.
The Harp still tastes reliably bitter;
I drop to the bottom of a puddle of slops

come up for air, watch the Karaoke clowns
force fifteen minutes fame from three minute wails.
Fatboy Slim spins on the juke box
as the strobes colourwash me into a Warhol cameo.
I spy a wink, or an eyelid collapsing
under pellets of caked black mascara.
She squeezes past so close that her breath
slaps my face. I say nothing, get a hard-on.

I've been there before and know how the song ends
– everyone sing-along now, play soldier,
elicit her name, where she's going to, coming from,
tell her you're sure you've met somewhere before,
loosen laughter with Bacardi Breezers,
chant second hand stories, then shimmy to the gents
and slip out the back door. It's simpler that way,
no embarrassed fumblings at last orders.

I'm under surveillance from too many lost souls
remembering when they were flesh and touched my flesh.
I sang an unholy duet with the banshee;
when you flirt with death's girl, there's no room for regrets.
The glass eyes fatten my reflection.
I hang in limbo in a hall of mirrors,

two-faced, half way to a peaceful universe;
I click my heels and stagger homewards

to kneel alone in the midnight silence,
savour the short staccato spasms
as I ease my fingers down my warm throat
move them in and out, in and out, faster now.
I fade from neon to ultraviolet,
watch dust motes circling in the jaundiced streetlight
that spills through the damp-ridden nets
on the window that's painted shut.

KEVIN HIGGINS

BORN IN LONDON IN 1967, GREW UP IN GALWAY CITY. HIS POEMS HAVE BEEN PUBLISHED IN METRE, THE SUNDAY TRIBUNE, ORBIS, THE SHOP, AND OTHERS THROUGHOUT IRELAND, BRITAIN AND THE UNITED STATES. HIS FIRST COLLECTION OF POETRY 'THE BOY WITH NO FACE' IS FORTHCOMING FROM SALMON POETRY. IN APRIL 2002 HE READ AT THE CUIRT INTERNATIONAL FESTIVAL OF LITERATURE. HE WAS A FOUNDING CO-EDITOR OF THE BURNING BUSH. HE HAS ALSO PUBLISHED REVIEWS AND ESSAYS.

A Brief History Of Those Who Made Their Point Politely And Then Went Home

On this day of tear-gas in Seoul
and windows broken at *Dickins & Jones*,
I can't help wondering why a history
of those, who made their point politely
and then went home, has never been written.

Those who, in the heat of the moment,
never dislodged a policeman's helmet,
never blocked the traffic or held the country to ransom.
Someone should ask them: "Was it all worth it?"

All those proud men and women, who never
had the National Guard sent in against them;
who left everything exactly as they found it,
without adding as much as a scratch to the paintwork;
who no-one bothered asking: "Are you or have you ever been?",
because we all knew damn well they never ever were.

By Five O'Clock

Your last day at the office gone down the drain,
you're null and void once again.
On Quay Street nothing but loud-mouthed money.
You live in a city – no a country –
run by idiots you went to school with.
Your father'd put his finger
precisely where you've gone wrong,
if he wasn't off in a mobile home
with her from number five.
But, in a week or so,
the up-side of idleness will strike you.
A universe of time for nothing but writing!
Your satires will suffer as you run out of characters
on a thin diet of teletext news.
Your girlfriend will dump you.
(Your lover won't phone.)
The blonde in the bookshop won't laugh at your jokes.
You'll visit your mother more and more often,
become what the girls at the office
call "the Norman Bates sort". Look in the mirror!
The smirk has slipped, Sunny Jim.
The face on the floor is definitely yours.

January
for Susan

The ashtrays need emptying
and the cat's been sick.
The mice in the attic are giving out stink.
As we watch our breath drift
across the kitchen, central heating
is a luxury as distant as trays
of oysters at the Galway Races.
The year struggles to its feet,
like a lamb stranded in deep snow.
Strange then to think, this evening in Siberia,
that these are the good old days;
I, the unknown "poet and critic",
you, the next F. Scott Fitzgerald,
up all night, putting the world to wrong;
writing new versions of old songs.

Estrangement: A Sequence

1. Till Agony Do Us Part
Just another suburban marriage,
it detonated and toppled in upon itself
rasing a frenetic smog of terminal
dust over the migraine sky.

Everyone saw it coming
after it had gone.

If it had a voice it would sound
like ghastly fingernails scraping
all the way down and across
the length and the breadth
of a shrieking blackboard.

2. She Looked Up
Looking up from the kitchen table,
her face withered with impressions of torn pictures,
faded photographs, archaic Christmas cards,
she eyeballed the mist on the window.

The poker faced clouds
had finally broken down.

A lonely pot of tea,
past its best,
kept her company.
They were meant for each other.

3. 3.19A.M.
There are ashes in the grate at this empty hour of the morning,
and unwashed plates fill the careless kitchen sink,
where the drip of the tap, it still insists.

Knives

It wasn't from the wind I took it:
with a grandad who once threatened
to tie a cat across the hedge,
so that nosy bastard neighbours, as they passed,
would gawk at it instead of in at him;
and a father who often likened
Albert Reynolds' face to a torn slipper;
I come from a long line of men,
who saw words not as decorations
but weapons, knives with which to cut
others down to size.

Letter To A Friend About Girls
after Philip Larkin

What losers we were when it came to girls.
'Pull up to my bumper baby, drive it in between'
played soundtrack to the wet dreams
of small, inconsequential fellas, the likes of us.
And we're talking small on an almost monumental scale.
In duffel coats and awful glasses
we shuffled around the edges of other people's parties
all through the eighties,
gawking down in the general direction
of our stupid, stupid shoes.
If charisma could be distilled,
ours would have been measured
in somewhat less than millilitres.
So small, we barely existed.

On the rare occasions when opportunity
- the tastiest variety - put herself there
to be availed of and there was nothing for it
but to press the advantage all the way home,
we either failed to spot the most obvious signals
- our radar were useless at picking incoming aircraft up -
or else managed to inexplicably miss.
She grinned through the worst jokes
and was clearly prepared to overlook that duffel coat,
but the score on the board stubbornly somehow stayed zero.
The goal could be yawning wide open
and still the ball would either trickle
pathetically wide or go sailing miles over.
And just what exactly were we supposed to say
as another cut-price night at The Oasis declined
(with no bachelor flat to which she might be lured back)?
"Let's explore the universe with my last fifty pence piece.
If I empty my pockets perhaps I could stretch as far as a kebab."

To Hell And Back Again

Now that, at last,
you seem to have found yourself
you often long to be lost again,
to drift down a throbbing street
in the thick of the afternoon
at the centre of your own solar system,
to shillyshally for hours
over a mug of tea and a slice of toast
in some greasy-spoon,
where no-one would even dream
of asking for a cappuccino or a latte,
or, better still, not to bother
leaving your filthy flat all day at all,
but, when the last ray of sun has, finally, gone away,
to shamble down to the kebab house
for a pickled onion and a portion of chips
because you don't have the cash
to use the brothel around the back.
But if you slip from these shackles,
your future which opens up
like a new continent that, of course,
must be conquered,
this clean living which sometimes fits you
like a collar and tie on a boiling hot day
at one of those awkward family occasions,
if you go back to all that liberty, to all that Hell,
you might not make it back again this time.

To Certain Lyric Poets

This lyric poet sees
his own reflection everywhere.
Even, 'her hair on the pillow
like freshly fallen snow',
is there to let us know
he still gets laid,
although, in this case,
she probably passed
through Robert Graves's hands first.
But we should be gentle
when we mention
"the narrowness of his range",
that lovely little phrase the critics invented,
a device to side-step saying, instead,
"he only ever talks about himself".
Every poem is another love-letter
to the person to whom
his whole life's work
has been dedicated.
He's been known
to agonise for hours
over a single word
and each one of them
is precisely meant
because, to him,
words are beautiful things,
flowers to be arranged
around an altar to his ego.

NIGEL McLOUGHLIN

Born in Enniskillen in 1968. His recent work has appeared in The Guardian and The Independent on Sunday and in literary journals in Ireland, UK, Japan, Belguim, USA and Australia. He has been twice short-listed for the Sunday Tribune/Hennessy Award and placed in the Kavanagh Award. His first collection 'At The Waters' Clearing' was published jointly by Flambard and Black Mountain Presses in 2001. He is currently finishing a second collection, 'Songs For No Voices'.

Forty Shades Of Fuchsia

I could show you three pictures from an old man's head.
I could show you that they lasted him a lifetime.
I could show you the last tree on an island
And the men breaking their boats to bury their dead.
I could show you a sky at evening.
I could show you forty shades of fuchsia.

I could show you bodies wasting into long shadows.
I could show you men dropping where they worked.
I could show you the road to no-where,
And where they say there is hungry grass.
I could show you a field of wild flowers.
I could show you forty shades of fuchsia.

I could show you a son standing over his father.
I could show you the grip slackening on his arm.
I could show you the plea in his eyes at his last words:
"Ná bí ag briseadh baidí ar bith domsa."
I could show you a host of boats at sail.
I could show you forty shades of fuchsia.

High Water

Day and daily, I have come to this ford
Loaded down with rag and ronian,
Have pitched them down and dowsed them,
And hopped them off the stones.
My fingers are flint and my palms
Sandpapered, cracked and hacked
From the constant hard water.

Day in and day out, I bring them:
Other peoples clothes, as my mother did,
As my young child will when I'm too old.
This is a family business.
I've cried, now and then, when the ache
In my hands gets too much or when
A hack cracks open and stains
Some new-washed garment red.

That's what happened yesterday –
As if I hadn't enough to do
Without washing simmets twice –
I was in tears, scrubbing and rinsing,
And working myself into a temper
As I lifted the clothing to the light
To check the stains had gone.
They caught me by surprise.

The leader gave me the strangest look,
I caught it out of the corner of my eye –
He turned sour-faced and pale.
I thought it better to be off –
Those men were trouble – I knew
Them from their South Armagh brogue.

I heard their leader died a short time later
Lashed to a pole with a crow on his shoulder,

And now the Ulstermen are saying I'm bad luck.
Come hell or high water, I'll be back again
Tomorrow, for there's another bundle ready
And you'll find me here, sousing
And dousing, wringing out the blood.

Butterfly's Bones

Mostly, they are hardly noticed
For they are too small or soft
To demand notice. They seem
To hide, shying from the gaze,
Shrinking from touch. Their recoil
Is instinctive. Yet their small voices
Roaring from the invisible are enough
To turn or cock a head like scent
In the breeze or an aftertaste.

Mostly, we don't look hard enough
Or tight enough to see them,
Our forkéd-ways vision dims
Them to denials, myths, lies.
Yet God is full of them, these
Tiny poems, and if we could only
Tune ourselves to hear the rattle
That photons make, taste heat
On the moving air, find the subtle
Scent of iron, see the spinning
Electron dance everywhere
And nowhere simultaneously

Or if we could touch, gently,
Gently, the insignificant
Butterfly's bones, then maybe,
Maybe we'd understand,
As children do, the last faint
And distant echoes of the voice
Of our once thundering God.

Song For No Voices

All the words I loved are gone,
Leaving me, mouth stopped,
With this slack tongue,
My jaw locked with rigor.
There are things left unsaid,
Of course, there always are,
On one side or the other.

But I remember how my
Outstretched arm would circle
The nape of your neck,
Your head lolling forward,
Full of sleep. The sweat
On the curls below your jaw,
A breast-brush on my thumb
That timed your breathing.

I remember feeling the foetus stir
Beneath your skin, under my limp
Hanging hand, how your turning
Legs encircled mine, hot tears
On my cheek and warm kisses.
It's these things I'm willing you
To remember, willing you to forget.

What's left to say? I left
Too quick, too quick, my love,
Like the turn of a kiss; left you
To batten down your grief with nails;
Give sorrow to the warm wood and
Tell our child, that I never knew,
I never knew.

Baile an Easa

She likes to go walking late at night
And the hooded figure that I pass
On the road might well be hers.

The laughing murder of crows amass
And almost break the branches
With dead weight. Burning sky blackens

Into monochrome. The middle ground
Becomes a series of gray shades.
Gorse burns. The moon drips, a rheumy

Eye through sackcloth, gibbous, changing
Like the pupil of a cat. It darkens
Off wet roofs where the glint of bulbs

Are moons in windows. The sodium light
Yellows everything, the tree, the house
The pillar of the road. Crossed by beams

Of a car, animal eyes redden in the night.
The moon has become a bull's eye,
Reddening in Taurus, unsilencing this place,

Loosing the hush and rush that named it
Once. The back of my neck quickens
Nerves goosepimple, hair stands. I feel

Shadows cross where there is no light.

Lines
for James McLoughlin

I

The lines were run in circles
Into boxes, measured out in yards,
Checking each hook and spanning
Breastbone to fist for the next,
Cursing the barb-bite of a stray.

The lines were lifted early, set late.
The time between, a fury of mending,
Checking, baiting, and driving drums
To the Dutchman to be weighed. Lunch
Was eels, fried still moving on the pan.

II

Lines of eels thrown lithe-live
Into an old oil drum in my uncle's boat.
Once, I tossed the drum, fell,
Screamed under their oozing mass
And always after fished for pike.

III

The little ones I carried home
Forefinger and thumb in either eye,
Larger ones were middle-finger
Gaffed under the last gill, taken
To be gutted, skinned and fried.

Jawbones of the biggest, boiled
And bleached, I kept for trophies.
With my fingers slashed by gills
Of one only stunned, I spent my summers
Dodging bailiffs and water-rats.

IV

Each assassin tempted out of reed-clumps
With live bait. Sink and draw, drawing out
The fight to complete capitulation on lines
Without trace-wire. My landing net was
A cold wet slapping on concrete piers.

V

Of the men who fished Lough Erne,
Professionally, few could swim
And none would fish at Whit.
It is said, the lough takes three
Lives every year, in memory

Of a sacrifice to the old god
Who lives two miles from shore
In the pit of the Broad Lough,
Where light stops and weights
Have failed to hit the bottom.

Even I, who stood on piers,
Threw lines where I would not go,
Pulled pike for fear of eels,
Even I stayed well away at Whit
Out of respect, fearing a slip.

VI

I've seen an eel cross land,
Snake its way to water with
A muscular will to live. Even
With the head cut off they thrash
For hours and if you poke a finger
Into the headless gullet, you can feel
The suck as it pulls towards the stomach.

VII

It's a peaceful death, they say,
But that's a lie that fishermen tell

To comfort relatives of the bloated
Corpse they drag, mangled from Lough
Gates or the net's mesh, mouths wide

In a watered scream, hands full
Of grass and weed they gripped so tight
The fingers must be broken to release it.
They say, you drown by thirds, three chances
To be caught and dragged thrashing back

To land, gulping air and fighting
For your life. Three breaths before
Water sucks your dream and thought
Dissolves, before everything is water,
Your eye wide and cold as the pike's.

VIII

I learned to swim
When I stopped fishing,
Left my singing reel
Left my line to rot.

The only thing I could not
Leave, the lough, the water,
Called me back as a mother
Would a straying child.

I never left it long. There
Is a bond of blood that pulls
Me to it: several ancestors
Dead by drowning.

IX

These days I run my lines by metre
Not the yard, but still I circle,
Box them in and check the hooks.
I run them shore to shore, have pushed
Apart the weight, the float and set
My lines to fish the deeper water.

NELL REGAN

NELL REGAN WAS BORN IN LONDON IN 1969 AND GREW UP IN DUBLIN. SHE HAS AN MA IN CREATIVE WRITING FROM THE POETS' HOUSE, DONEGAL AND LANCASTER UNIVERSITY AND HER FIRST COLLECTION OF POETRY, 'THE SIMPLICITY OF LEAVING', WILL BE PUBLISHED BY SALMON PRESS IN 2003. HER BIOGRAPHY OF HELENA MOLONY, 'TRADE UNIONIST AND REPUBLICAN', WAS PUBLISHED IN 2001 BY WOODFIELD PRESS IN FEMALE ACTIVISTS, IRISH WOMEN AND CHANGE 1900-1960.

Aspects of Prometheus (i)

I squint at the brave February sun
and try to gauge how he stole fire;
Did he approach the Vulcan's forge
with a fennel bulb grasped tight,
eyes watering from a molten lava
that exhaled with gloop and hiss?
Or perhaps it was a splinter of more
solid fuel he took, like they once
did here from a visited hearth.
Here, routine still centres on fire
which I awkwardly follow - bending over
the squat range to rake the ashes
first thing each morning, bringing
out warm cinders which gust towards
Muckish. Later, as I watch hot coal
glimmer and shoot stars in the slack,
I recall that fire only became
mortal when he brought it back,
mortal like us, and must be tended.

A Sense Of Place

I thought of you Dad,
when I heard the story of Colmcille
and `leac na cumhaidhe',
the stone of homesickness or loneliness.
`The lovely ladies of Iona' you'd say,
of the time the piano was there, with
those two old women in Dun Laoghaire,
their Georgian house by the sea
that had `Iona' inscribed above the door.
That black piano was so much a part

of our lives, brought from London
back to Cork, and every perilous
move after. That, and the endless
lectures on; how the Irish would
not listen to classical music,
how Dublin was not the real Ireland
anyhow, only the Pale. Funny that,
after all, it was London you missed,
symbol of all you despised. (I found
it hard to keep up sometimes.)

London, the terrain of your growing up,
and you had stories of close listening
to the radio for the late night broadcasts
from the Proms. Of getting cheap seats
at the old Vic and seeing `all the greats'
Gielguid, Olivier, eager to soak it all up.
Then, walking back to the small flat
on Sherland road where my grandparents
lived close-knit lives with those
they knew from Cork, and the church –

- all playing out a life of exile;
You'd been Cross Channel Dancing
champion at nine and Granny embroidered
intricate costumes for her blue-eyed son.
You told me once that it was seagulls
on the Thames broke your heart,
their lonesome cadence so far from sea.
That, if there was any animal you could be,
it would be a seagull, their clean white
shape so clear against the sky.

I think that was in Bray. Maybe walking
along the narrow path that wound around
the Head, where you'd christened all the spots;
The meander in the path from where
you could not see ahead or behind,
where the cliff sheered up on one side
and on the other, below the crumbling wall,
fell in a dizzying drop to the sea -
`the road to nowhere' you called it
I think, or was it `anywhere.'?

Soon after you left for Mayo and sold
the piano. With the money bought a small,
green ford - so you could get up to see
the three of us. (I had an image of you,
driving up and down, picking up unwary
hitchhikers, to interrogate on their politics
and why, oh why didn't they speak the Irish
language ? It made the journey shorter,
you said). But as for the piano, I felt
its loss, it was as though you'd given up

on Mozart, Scott Joplin and Bach;
`Johann Sebastian Bach', whose name
you pronounced with such care,

the 'fifth evangelist', and the only one
you'd kept faith with. Now instead, it was
'Dessie's flute', the heavy wooden one
and you struggled with traditional tunes.
In Mayo you'd stand outside the house,
facing toward the bay, pitching a tune
to an echo that called and called back to you.

After your death, I found the small notebooks,
hard-backed, with the names of hundreds of tunes
written in your careful hand, neatly listed
and categorised, by date or name or something
else. A wish for order so counter-pointed
by the way you lived your life. With these sits
the O'Neills and the flute, carefully wrapped
in a old towel, between them the large
D-whistle, your breath on aluminium
created its sweet, rasp of a sound

Ginestria

Voices are raised in old Pompeii, a polyglot babble
as legions of tourists march through narrow streets
and spill over into the Forum. We stand surrounded
by columns that rise to balmy air. "Here candidates
addressed the polis once" the guide shouts
over a clatter of kids racing past the grain mart.

The facts are; seventy two loaves burnt that noon
in a bakery; eight thousand people fled Pompeii
now daily this number returns; on Via d'Abundance
three women walk, raising dust on the stone footpath,
slowly crossing from one side to the other;
like jasmine the scent of a living town suffuses the air.

I suspect the two freed slaves, fortune made
in perfume, gaze down in delight (posterity assured)
as tours converge on their house, 1 Vicola dei Vetti,
and umbrella wielding guides jockey for position
to lead us through the frescoed walls. A red
born of sulphur, mercury, bursts out into the room.

In the cool marble bath house (after *aahhs* at
stucco ceiling and mosiac floor) we stare into glass
cases at two who did not survive the stinking gas;
all flesh and bone decayed, a vacuum of themselves
encrusted in a hide of ash, their last contortions
caught in plaster and become maquette. They are too

vulnerable there, caught in mid air. Do you think
they plead no longer with a falling sky of ash, lapilli
and stone so hot it is white but with us who stare?
We'd already climbed Vesuvias that day - peered into
its gaping maw, at smoke that issued from nearby rocks
and the yellow torrent of *ginestra* that streams toward Naples.

After The Funeral
i.m. Jimmy Simmons

After the funeral, night enters with a brief nod
then takes her leave again. I cannot sleep –

loose earth on your coffin still skitters in my head
and my feet walk me over the bog

a flat path winds through the emptiness
I could be the only person awake on earth.

Meadow sweet dust the air, vetch curl and trail,
wild iris stand tall in marshy pools and buttercups splay.

Hedges emerge and in the elderflower
a million white blooms confer.

On this wide expanse there is no grief, here
there is all grief and its only gesture is wildflower.

Light
for Caro

Light seeps through the curtains, blue-grey,
and over the thrum of my own thoughts
the high pitch of the dawn chorus,

sweet and insistent, reaches my ears.
I rise and pull clothes on,
I've given up on more sleep tonight.

It hardly gets dark in this place,
last night I pulled the curtains on an evening
that dawdled, reluctant to give way.

As I take my tea into the weakly lit yard,
(not night yet not day) I think of you
in Adelaide Street, a veteran of these early mornings.

The new moon hangs over the broad back of Muckish
and its less lonely to think that you may be up too,
padding blearily to the kitchen to put the kettle on

and half listen to the radio, preparing for these
long days of sun that are washing winter away.

COLETTE BRYCE

Colette Bryce was born in Derry in 1970. In 1995 she received an Eric Gregory Award and her work was introduced in 'Anvil New Poets 2'. Her first collection, 'The Heel of Bernadette', was published by Picador in 2000 and won the Aldeburgh Prize for Best First Collection and the inaugural Eithne and Rupert Strong Award. She lives in London.

Footings

You could see, for the life of you, no clear point
in monkeying seven, eight feet to the ground;
to slide from the belly, swing there (caught
by the arms, by the palms, by the fingertips), drop.
If I'd taken the trouble of minuses, pluses,
the length of the body, the height of the wall,
even pushed myself to prediction, scared you;
as it stood, before you leapt, I dared you.

And the lane it was yeared into two deep tracks
as we found our feet in the lengthened light,
for those with the leap approach to life,
for those who measure, look, think twice.
Both of us sobbing, I shouldered you home
with your hard-won knowledge, broken bone.

Break

Soldier boy, dark and tall, sat for a rest
on Crumlish's wall. *Come on over.*

Look at my Miraculous Medal.
Let me punch your bulletproof vest. *Go on, try.*

The gun on your knees is blackened metal.
Here's the place where the bullets sleep.

Here's the catch and here's the trigger.
Let me look through the eye.

Soldier, you sent me for cigs but a woman
came back and threw the money in your face.

I watched you backtrack, alter, cover
your range of vision, shoulder to shoulder.

Stones

We kept ourselves from children who were rich,
who were shaped in the folds of newest clothes,
who were strapped in the backs of foreign cars
whose quick electric windows rose
effortlessly, that poured into the stream of traffic;

but stared, fascinated, at their orthodontic
iron smiles, their nerve averted eyes.

They were quiet. They feared rain. They were taught
to recite in yellow rooms *Colette, Suzette,
Jo-jo and Lou are coming here for tea…*
or to sing from the prompt of a tuning fork
How merry your life must be…

They had no idea, but disappeared
to the South of France twice a year –
as we ran the streets, the lanes and squares,
robbers, outlaws, ne'er-do-wells –
then left for schools we didn't know.

From walls we saw them come and go.
War-daubed faces, feathers in our hair, wild,

we never smiled.

Young

Loose stacks of cassettes collapse
to the slam of the door behind us.
We take the stairs
in twos and threes,

we don't know where we might be
this time next year,
but meanwhile,
we apply to the future in lunch-breaks;

taste the possibility, the sweet adhesive
strip of A4 envelopes on tongues,
punch the day and run
to post, to home, and out.

We eye each other up as future lovers;
our faces smooth as blank maps
of undiscovered countries,
where only we might go.

We mean to go, we thumb the guides,
we spin the globe and halt it
at Calcutta, then Alaska, now Japan,
and plan. Imagine.

Not for us the paper lanterns of remember,
but the hard bright bulbs of sheer want.
We reminisce at length
about the future, which is better;

we harbour it in our hearts
like a terrible crush. We laugh
and drink to this in rented rooms.
We think Not this, but older, elsewhere, soon.

Owl

Watching, over ditch and field,
against a twisted, stricken tree,
tell us, tell us, what did you see,
what stretched your wild witness eyes,
what warped your song to this hoarse cry
of cruz, this unrelenting cry?
What shut your mind against the light,
what knowledge so eclipsed your life
as the sun turned her face away,
what binds you to the darkness
of that day?

I am net. Soul caught.
I am night swift instrument.
I am act borne of one thought,
blood must be atoned by blood.

Form

For some time I have been starving myself,
and not in the interest of fashion,
but because it is something to do
and I do it well.

I'm writing this as my only witness
has been the glass the wall.
Someone must know what I've done
and there's no one to tell.

Commitment is the main thing. After this,
the emptiness, the hunger isn't a sacrifice
but a tool. I found I was gifted, good.
And full of my vocation, sat or stood

at the mirror just watching my work
take shape, conform to my critical eye.
Or would lie, supine, stomach shrinking,
contracting, perfecting its concave line.

Each day gave a little more: depth to the shallows
of the temples, definition to the cheek,
contrast to the clavicle, the ankle bone, the rib,
the raised X-ray perception of my feet.

But one night I dressed and went for a walk
and felt a latent contamination of eyes
from windows and cars. I'd been feeling
strange, somehow encased, the hollow rush

of my own breath like tides in the shell
of my own head. A woman passed
and I saw myself in her glance,
her expression blank as a future.

The next day I woke to double vision,
everything suddenly terribly clear, only twinned.
My hearing, too, was distracted.
I sipped some water and retched.

My speech, when I test it, has stretched
to a distant slur like a voice from behind a door.
I would think I was losing my mind
if it wasn't behind all this from the start.

Tonight there's an almost imperceptible buzzing
in my bones, like the sound of electric razors,
a lawn-mower several gardens down.
I worry that they're crumbling

under my skin, dissolving like aspirin.
I worry that my bones are caving in.
When I sit my joints begin to set.
I try to stand and I'm hit by a shift in gravity,

the point where an aircraft lifts and enters flight.
And I think my sight is burning out.
I think it is losing its pupil heart.
Objects are calmly vacating their outlines,

colours slowly absorbing the dark.
In my dream the shovels uncover a hare,
preserved in its form, its self-shaped lair,
and I'm travelling in. There is no going back.

The Word

He arrived, confused, in groups at the harbours,
walking unsteadily over the gangways;
turned up at airports, lost in the corridors,
shunted and shoved from Control to Security;
fell, blinking and bent, a live cargo
spilled from the darks of our lorries,
dirty looking, disarranged, full of lies, lies,
full of wild stories, *threats and guns and foreign wars*
or He simply appeared, as out of the ground,
as man, woman, infant, child, darkening doorways,
tugging at sleeves with *Lady, Mister, please,
please...*

There were incidents; He would ask for it
with His crazy gestures, rapid babble, swaying
His way through rush hour trains, touching people,
causing trouble, peddling guilt in the market place,
His thousand hands demanding change, flocking
in rags to the steps of the church, milking
the faithful, blocking the porch, He was chased –
but arrived in greater numbers, needs misspelt
on scraps of paper, hungry, pushy, shifty, gypsy,
not comprehending *No* for an answer. What could we do?
We turned to the word. We called to our journalists,
they heard

and hammered a word through the palms of His hands, SCAM.
They battered a word through the bones of His feet, CHEAT.
Blood from a bogus crown trickled down, ran into His eyes
and His mouth and His throat, OUT.
He gagged, but wouldn't leave.

We rounded Him up with riot police,
drove Him in vanloads out of our streets,
away from our cities, into the tomb
and slammed the door on a job well done.
We are safer now, for things have changed:
we have laws in place like a huge, immovable stone,

should He rise again.

CAITRÍONA O'REILLY

Born in Dublin in 1973 and grew up in Wicklow. She was educated at Trinity College Dublin, where she wrote a Ph.D. on American Poetry. Her first collection, 'The Nowhere Birds' was published by Bloodaxe Books in 2001. She was awarded the 2002 Rooney Prize for Irish Literature.

On A Dropped Feather

Until the feather tapers like an arrow
it's a stem a hollow smoky glass
unsnappable from root to subtle tip.
A grounded starling could survive the loss.
    This ferny plumage where the shaft begins
is made of down too delicate for flight,
unlike the finny structure of the outer wing,
fashioned for soaring. Perhaps the taut
    intrinsic music of a bird comes
from the staves on its small fledged limbs.
The feather's utmost fibres have all the colour
and congruence of shot silk. From the loud strife
    and beating of wings in the sky somewhere
it fell like the notched blade of a knife.

Two Night Time Pieces

Pisces

Thirteen Februaries slept through
Before I learned what going under meant.

Pale and thin as sheets,
The near fields burst free of mooring.

Then the turn of the tide,
The sea stack,

The pier-light's onyx eye.
Those teenage dreams

Were cuttle-ink tattoos
Describing blue-rinse mermen,

Each muscular wave awash
With sex and phosphor.

I was awash and rocked,
Rocked hard to wake

And woke, drenched to the roots,
My flannelette pyjamas stiff with sand.

Sleep and Spiders

It is too strange to kill.
The symmetry of its eyes,

its eight paired legs askew
on the lintel, exoskeletal

and tiger-striped, all digestion.
It looks sudden but is still

for hours, eyes on stalks,
awaiting news from hair-triggers

that might be legs or fingers
(the whole thing a claw)

come to touch me in sleep–
hammock from which

black shadows seep.
Stars go milky, then go out.

I wake at five to what five is–
aA cold blue glow and a self

trussed, barely breathing,
paralytic with dreams.

Blueness

The dark sky of Switzerland
was the edge of the sky. Black metal from heaven
shed heavy radiance there and the air burned blue.
Glaciers glittered in the distance, inching south.
    There was blue in the mountain's throat.

After a six week thaw
foamy snow survived in the valley's angles.
The sun dropped from sight early and steeply.
In its electric shadow, blue-white storms
    scoured the tops of the hills.

And all things at first were blue.
It soaks the heart, fills the papery skin
of infants with vascular colour. This purplish hue
shadowing the hollow of my ribs tells again
    How cold and blue I am.

The Harbour In January

Maybe this landscape never frowned
and spoiled its early blue face.
Above, like an arched eyebrow,

a single crow makes broken circles.
Birds in the hedge confer in boiling voices.
It takes a large design to displace

mercury-heavy rolls like these-
water relaxing its folds of fabric.
It sees us bend from cockpit or quayside

and gives us shivering bodies, splintered
faces and hands. We aren't ourselves in it.
Like a glamorous uncrossed desert,

this sea's of mobile feature. Any ship's legacy
is a smile that widens and complicates
and gapes to take in all the bay and me-

not of the sea, not in it, just looking on
at how the purple undertow reveals itself
in surfacing, in lapsing platinum.

Autobiography

Here the weather has its own spectrum,
a seemingly limitless palette. To the north
a chain of swollen, dark green mountains.
Mostly they are smooth and stippled with heather,
then too I've seen them snow-capped, gleaming.
The run of mountains ends with the seaward
drop of Bray Head's ponderous mossy forehead.
Between there and here are miles of salty fields.
Clattering by on the littoral track after a flood
 I've seen the miserable cattle islanded
on the high ground of their uneven fields.
In summer those meadows burn with gorse.
An intermittent shot to scare the birds
is all that disturbs the gelatinous air–
that, and the odd vertical string of bonfire smoke.
The distant hill on which my town is built quivers.
I live between three Victorian piers on the bay's industrial side.
The bay smiles, it is full of flattened shiny water
sucking quietly at the shore and piers. All night
I adjust my own breath to its eternally regular breaking.
Less frequently now, a cargo ship sets up
a prehistoric rumble in the waters of the bay
and docks, raising its hatches with a metal groan.
Two synchronized forklift trucks neatly stack
the planks of timber, balletic and mechanical.
When ships brought raw cement, plumes of dust
would sweep across the bay, coating our windows and doors.
On the east side of my house is an ancient castle keep
of blackest rock, that leans like a fin
from the back of the sea. I live in the shadow
of the shadow of a castle's walls.
They have fallen to hummocks of bright grass
that we played in as children,

wriggling into nests and hidey-holes.
The dark beach in the lee of the castle
is where Saint Patrick put ashore. He soon left,
Shocked at the native's epic unfriendliness:
They knocked Saint Manntan's front teeth down his neck.
Among the shells and shingle of the beach
are opalescent nuggets of glass, rounded and stone-smooth
from aeons rolling on the ocean floor.
Was it really from wrecked galleons they came?
But still there is the bay's omega, its theatre of weather,
a glass bowl for the sky to play in. The sea has no colour
save what weather brings. I've watched the sky and sea
go up in flames at dusk, though mostly they're an angry grey.
Now any horizon of mine must be nine-tenths sky.

MARY O'DONOGHUE

BORN IN 1975, IS FROM CO. CLARE. HER POETRY AWARDS INCLUDE SEAN DUNNE YOUNG WRITER AWARD, AND THE INAUGURAL SALMON POETRY PRIZE FOR HER FIRST COLLECTION 'TULLE'. SHE IS THE 2001 HENNESSY/SUNDAY TRIBUNE NEW IRISH WRITER FOR HER SHORT FICTION. HER POETRY APPEARS IN IRISH, US, AUSTRALIAN, CANADIAN AND BELGIAN PUBLICATIONS. IN SUMMER OF 2003, SHE WILL TAKE UP A RESIDENCY AT VIRGINIA CENTRE FOR CREATIVE ARTS, AWARDED BY THE TYRONE GUTHRIE CENTRE.

The Textures
for John C

I am velvet.
Smooth nap,
But rub me up the wrong way
And I bristle,
Growing hackles
Beneath your palms.

I am moiré.
Metallic skin,
But scan me
Under lamplight,
See silk
Shot through
With routes of tears.

I am tulle.
Lively bustle,
But gather me
Between your hands,
I rustle,
Murmur,
Settle.

Jezebel's Palms

In the Bible, Jezebel was thrown to the dogs for her immorality.
They ate everything but for the palms of her hands.

Oh, we all saw what happened
To Jezebel. Her come-uppance
Was partly an example to us
Townswomen.
A gorey alert to the hazards
Of torrid bedrooms
And snake-tangled limbs.

The last thing we saw
From inside the wall
Were her long-nailed toes
Dragging furrows in the red clay.
Eight dogs lolloped into the trees
With their unexpected bait.
Her face was already skinned
Off, chipped on the edges of steps
And peeled in pink strips
Against the rocks' uneven teeth.
(The dogs came back to snuffle up
These traces of face, their lips
And whiskers enamelled hard
With dark-dried blood).

None of our eyes met
After that morning. I forced
Myself to go there a week later
To gather some roots for a
Poultice, and diced round
Red-dyed plots on the forest ground.
I doubled over to haul up a brown

Knobbled root. A soggy leaf
Clung to my palm and I unpeeled
It and doubled over again to vomit
Yellow, green peas and cabbage shreds
Into the undergrowth. The leaf,
A red palm on mine, curling up
In the breeze. I found its match
And pocketed them both
And smoothed out the paper-thin
Fingers all the way home.

In front of my candle's light,
A pair of palms smoulder
See-through red. Lines divide
On and out, as thin
And infinite as cobweb threads.
I lick some cat's gut
For my needle and press
Palm to palm. I puncture them
Near where the wrist used to be
And start to stitch
The way round, looping up
And down thumb and each
Finger, and finish with a knot
Of gut and a snip.

My hand crawls
Into this slippery flesh glove
And lies fastened
Between the palms
Of Jezebel. Translucent
Top-stitched wafers,
Meaty,
Indigestible.

The She-Machines

A Ship is a She.
Is this because she
Makes a fine vessel,
Wombing Lilliputian people
In her iron crannies?

As a young one,
Her sails are a multiple bosom,
Wobbling and ballooning nobly
Until she is smashed in the planes
Of her angular face
With a bottle
And made to sever the water.
Maiden's Voyage

The Car.
Her auto-biography has not been
Written. But you'd need
Some class of a manual
To diagnose the irascible moods
Of this caboose.
Sometimes in the winter
She has a minor breakdown
(Seasonal Affective Disorder)
And stubbornly refuses to churr.
But nothing that can't be remedied
By tipping back her bonnet
And smoothing out the vexed nubs
Along her spark-plug nerves.

The six-hundred pound
Mincing Machine squats
Fat and in a pock-marked suit

Of Hammerite. She volleys
Out sossies like a chain
Of limbless babies.
Hourly gorging on the forced
Pink mess, butting it out sheathed
From her churning belly-bag.
She feels the buyer ogling
Her brawny fork and slapping
Her cold shanks with a price.

Haughty bitches.
Hellbent Hitachis skirt
Their amber armour in
Mucky brown kerfuffles
By cavorting through flash-floods.
They need a certain vanity.
To make up for the birth-defect.
One-armed, but protracted use
Has steeled a ruthless clasp.
Sometimes, dangling a Port-A-Loo
Aloft from her finger prong,
She strikes an attitude
Of half-come-hither worship
To the crane,
Her yellow crucifix menacing
The crop of sprouting houses.

Lavoisin and Lavigoreux

French midwives, fortune-tellers and poisoners of the late 17th century

They tickled the gills
of death-cups and stinkhorns
and pestled the poison
from hemlock and bracken,

then up the stairs
to gab incantations
and raddle their hands
in raw labour rooms,

back to the roking stewpot
to brew some little heart-block
with a *soupcon* of hallucination
for husbands of wives with patience,

apothecaries bleeding wild cherries,
to cripple him more: 'false hellebore';
finish the deed with broiled jimsonweed.

Their hands were still fragranced
with cocklebur mulch
when the molten poker
put holes through the palms,

their hands were lopped off
and dropped to the cobbles,
they kindled like twin torches
in the nightshaded Place de Gréve.

Bova

I

When my mother passed on I was forty-four,
Left to live in the corner
Of a clammy screaking house.
Master of cattles and grasses,
Bank-shy, with my stooks of notes
Insulating the loft.
What I needed was a class of a woman.
A creature to stop me
Being swallowed by mildew and stale brack and yellowed vests,
The bulky stench of my fumbled cooking.
Baffled longing rose off me like a gas.
I was sixty miles down the country,
Speculating on scrawny yearlings.
When she careened into her father's yard
See-sawing between two buckets.
Eighteen at the most, in a child's cheerful apron
Fastened in the muck by big contorted wellingtons.

II

Jesus, what else was I going to do?
Sheep were selling for a pound
My wife in St. Vincent's remnants.
Scarcity hauled down our pride
Like a concrete block on a rope.
Who else was going to ask for her?
The village used to snigger at something
In her jiggering eyes,
So we kept her to ourselves
And tacked chicken-wire to her window.
When we saw the money fanned out
In the visitor's bartering hands,

My wife sucked it into her mouthy O
And I let the girl go

III

He said he didn't mind if my look
Swivelled like the navy eyes of a cow
Twisting in their milky scope.
I watch mould frilling outwards like neck-bruises
On the ceiling when he lurches over on me.
I can't remember the price
Of my hefty sixteen-year frame.
In his house I am queen of hens and rhubarb,
Rewarding the quietness with a pluck of my ear.
His whisky friend smeared my cheeks and mouth
With a beef lick of his blubbering tongue.
Where was my mother
When men haggled for me?
A hanky triangled her face
And she burned off scutch grass,
Charring little pieces
Of our shared women's faces.

IRISH LANGUAGE INTRODUCTION

Selecting Irish language poets and poems for this anthology, I have kept to the general editors' remit of only including poets who are new kids on the block of Irish poetry, even though one or two of them may have published more than one collection. Publication of more than one volume in Irish was not, in my view, sufficient grounds to bar a writer from this anthology. My reason is that poets in Irish tend to be all but invisible to the great Irish, and wider, public until they have published approximately three books in Irish and, usually, one bilingual or English language selection. Sin mar atá / that's just the way it is, although I often find myself wishing that Irish readers were as plurilingual as Irish writers and writing tend, generally and historically, to be.

The poets featured here are part of the post-*INNTI* generation, standing on the shoulders of such literary giants as Nuala Ní Dhomhnaill, Michael Davitt, Cathal Ó Searcaigh, Liam Ó Muirthile and others. They bring their own twist to the tale, and tail-end, of twentieth century poetry in Irish as it swings into the twenty-first century. Celia de Fréine is a remarkable writer in her own write (as John Lennon would say) but also as a bilingual author, managing to find *le mot juste* and just the word in two languages. In the middle of the last century, Eoghan Ó Tuairisc remarked that the bilingual author is not trusted by either camp; currently, de Fréine is winning accolades from both the Irish and English language 'camps' for a transgressive poetry that has a dancing and sometimes arse-kicking foot in both camps.

Gearóid Mac Lochlainn is gaining increasingly widespread recognition for the quality and musicality of his work. Following on from Pól Ó Muirí, he has brought the personal and shared, previously unwritten, experiences and perspectives of the urban Belfast modern gaeilgeoir / Irish speaker into the light and unto the page. He has done so with style but also sincerity, writing about subjects (public and private, personal and political) that leave most dumb or up dead-ends. His achievement so far is remarkable, and his work deserves the same description that Ní Dhomhnaill once gave to the work of Ciarán

Carson: it is 'alive-alive-oh'. True and close to life, Gearóid's poems still manage to dance, sing and be airborne partly because they are informed by an attentive reading of, and listening-in to, these and other sources: the rhythms and patterns of everyday speech (Irish and English); the craft and irreverence of the Beats; the drums and voices of Native American and other tribal societies; the jamming and mixing of reggae and reels; the harmonics and dynamics of macaronic writing from here to Italy.

Colette Ní Ghallchóir, Tarlach Mac Congáil and Mary Reid are newer voices to me, voices that I am still registering and tuning in to. Already they promise much in themselves and for the future of poetry in Irish, a poetry that is remarkably diverse in subject matter and style. Each of these three poets show strong signs of transmuting, in Seamus Heaney's phrase, 'feeling into words', but also of surprising the reader with poems that aren't just about experiences, but actually are experiences in themselves (as Seán Ó Ríordáin and, later, Eavan Boland recommended).

Poetry in Irish may be thought of as a small pond dominated by a few big fish such as Ní Dhomhnaill, Ó Searcaigh and a few others whose work is also published in bilingual editions. However, the pond is well worth further exploration. From its depths in recent years, much of the best of Ireland's poetry has emerged.

Frank Sewell

CELIA DE FRÉINE

CELIA DE FRÉINE IS A POET, DRAMATIST, AND SCREENWRITER. ORIGINALLY FROM CO. DOWN, SHE NOW DIVIDES HER TIME BETWEEN DUBLIN AND CONAMARA. MANY OF HER PLAYS HAVE BEEN PRODUCED INCLUDING MOST RECENTLY NÁRA TURAS È IN AISTEAR BY AMHARCLANN DE HÍDE IN 2000. HER TELEVISION WORK WAS SHORTLISTED FOR THE CELTIC FILM AND TELEVISION FESTIVAL (1998). HER POETRY HAS WON MANY AWARDS, INCLUDING THE PATRICK KAVANAGH AWARD (1994), DUAIS CHOMÓRTAS FILÌOCHTA DHÚN LAOGHAIRE (1996), THE BRITISH COMPARATIVE LITERATURE ASSOCIATION TRANSLATION AWARD (1999), AND DUAIS AITHEANTAIS GHRADAM LITRÍOCHTA CHLÓ IAR-CHONNACHTA (1999). SHE WAS AWARDED ARTS COUNCIL BURSARIES IN 1997 AND IN 2000. A COLLECTION 'FAOI CHABÁISTÍ IS RÍONACHA' WAS PUBLISHED BY CLÓ IAR-CHONNACHTA IN 2001. THE ATTACHED POEMS ARE FROM A COLLECTION IN HAND ENTITLED 'FIACHA FOLA' WHICH IS AN EXPLORATION OF THE BLOOD SCANDAL. CELIA PROVIDES HER OWN TRANSLATIONS FOR THE POEMS WHICH FOLLOW.

Mochthráth an Mhic Tíre

Fiafraíonn an speisialtóir díom
an bhfuil aon eolas agam faoi *lupus*.

Freagraím gur bhásaigh
cara liom dá bharr. Dar leis

ní bhásaíonn éinne
dá bharr sa lá atá inniu ann.

Bhí mé ag a sochraid
am ar cuimhin liom a deirfiúr ag rá

gur dhúirt a liasa nach mbaineann
daoine a bhfuil *lupus* orthu

meán an tsaoil amach.
Molann mo dhuine cortasón –

stéaróideach a atann an corp
go bhfios dom. Samhlaím mé féin

i riocht mná *Michelin* ar foluain
os a chionn ag breathnú anuas

ar mhaoil a chloiginn
fad is a fhuineann sé mo bholg.

The Hour of the Wolf

The specialist asks
if I've heard of *lupus*.

I tell him a friend
died from it. *No one*

dies from lupus
nowadays, he says.

I was at her funeral
when her sister mentioned

that their specialist had said
that people with *lupus*

do not reach middle age.
He prescribes cortisone –

a steroid I've heard that bloats
the body. I see myself

in the guise of a *Michelin*
woman float up overhead

stare down on his pate
as he pummels my stomach,

Comhthionól

Cheap siad go raibh siad
tar éis an dallamullóg a chur orainn
go raibh muid chun suí siar
is glacadh leis an bpraiseach.

Ní raibh siad ag súil
go dtionólfadh muid cruinnithe
go gcuirfeadh muid fios ar shaineolaí
as ospidéal i Sasana

a bhí tar éis fainic
a chur ar an mBord Fola.
Tá sé iontach
agus scanrúil.

Níl mé in ann fanacht
sa halla ban seo níos mó
is éisteacht leis an gcaoi
ina dtolgfaidh caoga faoin gcéad againn

aicíd amháin is fiche faoin gcéad aicíd eile.
Níl mé in ann breathnú tharam
is na figiúirí seo a leagan
ar éadain mo chompánach.

Lobby

They thought they'd
got away with it –
that we were going
to sit back and accept this mess.

They hadn't expected us
to summon meetings
to have a specialist flown in
from a hospital in England

that had already
warned the Blood Bank.
It is wonderful
and awful.

I can no longer sit
in this hall of women
and listen to how
fifty per cent of us will develop this

and twenty per cent that.
I can no longer look
around me and transfer
these facts to faces.

Ag tástáil, ag tástáil...

Bíonn blas an Tuaiscirt le cloisteáil ar chaint
mo rogha fleibeatamaí, báine an tsneachta
le feiceáil ar a gúna mar aon lena bróga,
calóga aol na hoíche aréir á scaipeadh aici.

Is ar a hiallacha fada tanaí a bhreathnaím
nuair a deir sí: *cuir do lámh ar mo ghlúin.*
Ceanglaíonn banda gorm thar mo bhícéips.
Dúnaim is scaoilim mo dhorn go mbraithim

go bhfuil mo lámh ar tí pléascadh is go seasann
mífhéitheoga amach ar nós na sruthán puitigh
a bhíonn le feiceáil is mé ar eitilt thar Shasana.
Is cliste iad a méara, dea-chóirithe a fiala. Gorm
is dearg is glas a gclaibíní. M'ainm go léir ar a lipéid
iad á leagan i bplaisteach aici lena lámhainní rubair.

Testing, testing...

My favourite phlebotomist speaks with
a Northern accent. Her dress is white. So
too are her shoes. I can tell from the flakes
that she whitewashes them at dead of night.

I stare at her laces when she says *Put
your hand on my knee.* She ties a blue band
around my biceps. I clench and unclench
my fist till my arm feels like it's going

to burst and my veins stand out like the maze
of Slobland streams seen when flying over
England. Her fingers are deft. Her vials
neatly ordered. Lidded in blue and red
and green and purple. Clearly labelled and
placed in plastic by her rubber-gloved hands.

A leannáin

Ní mholfainn d'aon long leaba ancaire
a lorg sa chuan sin thall ar eagla
go loitfeadh na tocsainí a droimlorga:

agus an ghealach lán tonnann smugairlí róin
ar uachtar a n-adharcáin ullamh acu; in aice
na sceire ionsaíonn sliogánaigh leathmharbha a chéile;

thíos ar an ngrinneall ábhraíonn bairillí.
Cá bhfios nach ndéanfar smidiríní astu
amach anseo is nach bpléascfar a bhfuil iontu?

A leannáin, fan amach uaim.

Lover

It is no longer safe to enter this harbour –
toxins in the water could damage
the hull of any ship dropping anchor here:

when the moon is full jellyfish surge to the surface,
tentacles at the ready; beside the reef
half-dead molluscs attack each other;

and on the sea bed barrels fester.
In years to come they may shatter –
their contents explode.

Lover, keep your distance.

A Dheirfiúracha Dílse
i ndiaidh Marina Tsvetaeva

Mo léan, níor éirigh linn éalú as Ifreann
cé gur ghlac muid lena raibh i ndán dúinn,
na dualgais a roinneadh orainn.

Ní sinne a mealladh
ó chliabháin ár ngasúr
go tinte cnámh na mbligeard.

Ag cromadh chun na gcliabhán céanna
chomh naíonda leis na naíonáin iontu
b'iad na bligeaird a théaltaigh aníos chugainne.

Is maith is eol daoibh, a bhanabhraiseacha,
gur den scoth ár dtíos, is nach dúinn
is dual clú sa drochobair snáthaide.

Cén mhaitheas dúinn samhlú
sna hoícheanta gan suan
céard a tharlódh dá mbeadh

an dara rogha againn –
dá ndamhsóimis nocht faoi na réaltaí
an gcinnfí an cháin chéanna orainn?

Is tirim iad ár súile.
Bíonn ár n-aenna de shíor á gcnaí.
Thit an ghruaig dár gcloigne.

Sracadh an fheoil dár gcnámha.
Go deimhin, a dheirfiúracha dílse,
níor éirigh linn éalú as Ifreann.

Dear Sisters
(after Marina Tsvetaeva)

We have not escaped hell
though we had accepted our lot,
the chores apportioned to us

nor were we lured
from the cradles of our children
to bonfires lit by vagabonds.

As we leaned over those same cradles
innocent as the children in them
the vagabonds crept up to us.

Never fear, fine spinners,
good housekeepers –
it is not we who are renowned

for slovenly needlework;
nor is there any point thinking
during those sleepless nights

what hand fate would have dealt us
had we not accepted our lot –
had we danced naked under the stars

would we have been punished just the same?
Our eyes are dry, our livers gnawed,
hair has fallen from our heads,

flesh has been clawed from our bones.
Definitely, dear sisters,
we have not escaped hell.

Lámhachta?

Go deireanach istoíche
nuair nach féidir liom
titim im chodladh
nó nach féidir léamh
nó nach leor drón Leonard Cohen
le mé a leagan amach
breathnaím ar scannáin.

Cloisim gur fir bhriste iad
lucht na gcótaí mbána
nach féidir leo titim
ina gcodladh ach oiread.
Meas tú céard a bhíonn
ar siúl acusan go
deireanach istoíche?

An gcaitheann siad
a gcuid ama i gcuideachta
Cohen nó ag breathnú
ar scannáin – ina suí ina dtithe
ar a dtoilg ag breathnú
ar na scannáin chéanna
a mbímse ag breathnú orthu?

Go minic feicim fir
cúlpháirtithe i gcoireanna
nár lean iarmhairtí
chomh trom céanna iad
á sracadh as a leapacha
is á lámhachadh.
An bhfuil mé ag iarraidh

go gcaithfí mar an gcéanna
le dream na héagóra seo?
Nó arbh fhearr liom
go mairfidís
i liombó d'aicídí?
Níorbh fhearr.
Ní ghuífinn a leithéid ar éinne.

Taken out and shot?

Late at night when I can't sleep
or can't read, and even
the drawl of Leonard Cohen
isn't enough
to knock me out
I watch films.

I hear that the men
in white coats
are broken men
who can't sleep either.
I wonder what they do
late at night?

Do they spend time
in the company of Cohen
or do they watch films
in their houses on their settees –
do they watch
the same films as me?

I have seen films
where men were dragged
from their beds
and shot for less

than what these did.
Would I like to see these

culprits suffer
the same fate? Or would
I prefer them to live
in a limbo of ailments?
No.
I wouldn't wish that on anyone.

GEARÓID MAC LOCHLAINN

Gearóid Mac Lochlainn was born in Belfast in 1967. He is a musician and songwriter with the Irish language world-music group Bréag; and also broadcaster with the Irish language section of BBC N. Ireland. To date, he has published three volumes of poetry: 'Babylon Gaeilgeoir' (Belfast: An Clochán, 1997); 'Na Scéalaithe' (Dublin: Coiscéim, 1999); and, most recently, a bilingual collection, 'Sruth Teangacha' / 'Stream of Tongues' (Indreabhán: Cló Iar-Chonnachta, 2002). The latter text features an introduction by Nuala Ní Dhomhnaill, and translations into English by Ciarán Carson, Medbh McGuckian and other leading poets. In recent years, Gearóid has won numerous major awards for his work.

Daoine nach luaitear
(do mo dhá chara)

Agus sibhse!
Sibhse nach luaitear i ndánta,

na daoine nach bhfaigheann tiomnú
'do' nó 'for' nó fiú 'i ndílchuimhne' is an t-am ann,

sibhse nach ndéanann ábhar dáin,
nach fiú sibh ar a laghad haikú bídeach,

sibhse nach luaitear,
atá ró-ró-chóngarach,

bainigí na dallóga de bhur súile.
Amharcaigí istigh.

Nach bhfeiceann sibh gur
sibhse ábhar an fhíorchaointe,

cúis na díomá,
foinse na mbriathra,
an crann taca?

Sibhse an spreagadh.

Unsung Heroes
(for my two friends)

And you!
You who don't get a mention in poems;

who never get a dedication
'to', 'for' or, when the time comes, 'in memoriam';

you who don't make it into poems,
don't you deserve a haiku, even?

You who go without saying,
who are too ... too close to home,

open your eyes,
catch yourselves on.

Don't you see
you're the stuff of poems,

the cause of laments,
the source of the words,
the foundation and support?

You, my friends,
are the inspiration.

(trans. by Frank Sewell)

Aistriúcháin
(Léamh filíochta, Meán Fomhair 1997)

The act of poetry is a rebel act - Michael Hartnett

Ní aistriúcháin a chloisfidh sibh anocht, a chairde,
mé aistrithe, athraithe is caolaithe
le huisce aeraithe an Bhéarla,
a dhéanfadh líomaneaid shúilíneach
d'fhíon dearg mo chuid filíochta.
Ní bheidh mé aistrithe anocht.
I mean like, cad chuige a bhfuil mé anseo
ar chor ar bith?

An ea gur seo an faisean is úire –
léamh dátheangach, *poetry* as Gaeilge?
An ea go bhfuil an saol ag athrú?
Ní féidir a bheith cinnte.
Amanna, éiríonn tú tuirseach
de chluasa falsa Éireannacha.
Féinsásamh an monoglot a deir leat –
'It sounds lovely. I wish I had the Irish.
Don't you do translations?'.

Iad ag stánadh orm go mórshúileach
mar a stánfadh ar éan corr a chuireann
míchompord de chineál orthu.
Iad sásta go bhfuil sé thart,
sásta go bhfuil an file Béarla ag teacht i mo dhiaidh
le cúpla scéal grinn
a chuirfidh réiteach ar an snag seo san oíche.

Agus seo é anois againn
lena achuid cainte ar *'café culture'* agus *'Seamus'*.
Seo é le cruthú dóibh go bhfuil siad
leathanaigeanta is cultúrtha,

go dtuigeann siad an pictiúr mór,
go dtuigeann siad filíocht.
Seo anois é.

Agus sin mise ansiúd thall i m'aonar,
i gcoirnéal mo ghruaime,
ag stánadh go héadmhar,
ólta ar fhíon rua mo chuid filíochta,

mo chuid filíochta Gaeilge
nár thuig éinne.

Translations
(Poetry reading, September 1997)

'The act of poetry is a rebel act'—Michael Hartnett

Tonight, my friends, there will be no translations,
nothing trans-lated, altered, diluted
with hub-bubbly English
that turns my ferment of poems
to lemonade.
No, tonight, there will be no translations.
'Séard atá á rá agam ná',
what am I doing here anyway?

Is this just the latest fashion, a fad –
the bilingual reading,
poetry *'as Gaeilge'*?
Had the world gone mad?

Sometimes, you get tired talking
to lazy Irish ears. Tired

of self-satisfied monoglots who say
'It sounds lovely. I wish I had the Irish.
Don't you do translations?'

There they are, gawping at me, wide-eyed,
like I'm some kind of odd-ball
just rolled out of lingo-land,
making them all uneasy.
And how glad they are when it's over,
glad the 'English' poet is up next
with a few jokes to smooth over
the slight hitch in the evening.

And here he is
with his talk of 'café culture' and 'Seamus'.
Here he is to prove to them
they are witty, broad-minded, and cultured;
that they get the gist of this poetry thing,
that tops and tails the evening.
Here he is now.

And there's me in the corner,
alone, dejected,
gawping wide-eyed with jealousy,
drunk on the red wine of my poetry,

my 'Irish' poetry
that no-one understood.

(trans. by Gearóid Mac Lochlainn and Frank Sewell)

Rogha an Fhile

Táim i dteannta ag fadhb Shíneach na teanga seo -
an Ghaeilge.
Cad chuige a meallann sí mé?
Níor tógadh mé léi.
Ní cainteoir líofa mé fiú
(cibé rud é sin).

Ach mealltar mé
mar mheisceoir meidhreach chuig cúlán ceoil
nó seisiún rúnda a bhfuil leid le tabhairt
chun fáil isteach.
Cad tá le deeanamh? Tá mé i bponc.
Níl an t-am agam le bheith ag slogadh siar foclóir
ná an chleasaíocht agam
le blas na Gaeltachta a bhrú ar mo chuid cainte,
is níl an fonn orm bheith gafa i ndianchúrsa eile
le lucht meánaicme Bhaile Átha Cliath.

Tabhair *break* dom, a chara.

Is céard faoin cheird seo,
bua na filíochta?
Admhaím don domhan gur fearr liom Ó Dónaill ná Dineen.
Is tá an saol gairid, róghairid le bacadh
lena leithéid de shean-Ghaeilge, meán-Ghaeilge,
filíocht shiollach, meadaracht
is an tíoránach dorcha sin, rófhada sa diallait - Traidisiún.

Cut to the chase,
ní féidir liom sheasamh os bhur gcomhair
lán och och ón is och ón ó.
Foc sin faoi dhó!

Ba mhian liom labhairt gan chosc, gan cheangal.
Ach cad is fiú é mura n-éisteann tú?

Fágtar ar an trá fholamh mé,
idir dhá chomhairle,
idir dhá thine Bhealtaine
is b'fhéidir idir cúpla seanfhocal eile
nach bhfuil ar bharr mo theanga.

The Poet's Choice

I'm in a fix with this Chinese puzzle of a tongue -
Irish.
Why does it fret me?

I wasn't raised with it,
I'm not even a fluent speaker
(whatever that is).

But I'm lured like some lost reveller
to a lock-in session
where only abracadabra and winks
can open the door.
What's to be done?
I haven't the time to cram dictionaries.
nor the conceit to forge a Gaeltacht slant
onto my speech.
And I don't fancy
another 'vocational course'
with a bunch of Dublin 4s.

Gimme a break, *a chara*.

And what about this poetry thing?
This easy flow of words?

I'll tell you now for nothing
that I go for Ó Dónaill, not Dineen
and that life's too short to get hung up,
on Old Irish, Middle Irish,
syllable and metre,
and that long-in-the-tooth old hag -
the traditional thing.
I can't stand here lowing the
Och Och on either.

I want to speak, rant, rave,
untie tongue till it blooms and bleeds
in seven shades of street rhythms.
But you're not listening again, are you?

So I'm left high and dry,
up shit creek,
between a rock and a hard place,
the devil and the deep,
and some other old chestnut
that's choking me up.

(trans. by Gearóid Mac Lochlainn and Frank Sewell)

Brionglóid dheireannach Chrazyhorse

He had seen what happened to the chiefs who went to the Great father's house in Washington; they came back fat from the white man's way of living and with all the hardness gone out of them.... Now the white man had bought Little Big Man and made him into an agency policeman.
As Crazyhorse walked between them, letting the soldier chief and Little Big Man take him ... he must have tried to dream himself into the real world to escape the darkness of the shadow world in which all was madness.
(Dee Brown)

I

Scéal liom daoibh.

Crainn bheannaithe
ar shroich a ngéaga na spéartha
leagtha is athdhéanta ina mílte
teachíní bídeacha.

Aibhneach soilseacha, gnaíúla
anois deargdhubh
le putóga na gCnoc Dubh.

Bláir fhairsinge, gleannta doimhne,
roinnte ina mílte
gairdíní cúnga.

Éanacha an aeir
imithe thar farraige,
uibheacha an iolair
briste ina smionagar.

Mac tíre tostach
roimh ghealach fhuar, fhuilteach.

Dromanna na gcapall fiáin
lúbtha ag diallait
an chríostaí ramhair.

Cíocha torthúla, boga na mban
clúdaithe roimh fhealsúnacht
an tseanmóirí.

Déithe ársa mo chine
curtha ag eaglais
an tsagairt.

Guaillí crua, bródúla mo chairde
clúdaithe le cótaí gorma
an airm.

Laochra fiáine, uaisle
a throid go cróga ag mo thaobhsa
mar phuipéid an uisce bheatha.

Cnámha ag síneadh
trí chraiceann ghnúis
linbh shnoite

le linn do na mílte buabhall
bheith ag lobhadh
in aer teasaí an bhláir fholaimh.

II

Is cad a dhéanfadh Crazyhorse
dá mairfinn?
Cá rachfainn san fhásach seo?
Cá bhfaighinn faoiseamh?

C'áit a gcluinfinn amhránaí
ag canadh faoi na seanchogaí?

nach bhfuil siad tostach
roimh scréach na ngunnaí?

Is c'áit a gcluinfinn
an druma álainn ag bualadh?

Nach bhfuil siad balbh
roimh thormán na gcos
ag mairseáil?

Is c'áit a gcluinfinn
teangacha milse, míne
na Sioux, Cheyenne, Apache?

Nach bhfuil teanga an choinmhthígh
ar a mbéalaibh?

Tá gach rud imithe,
tá an domhan ag druidim.
Níl ann ach brionglóid,
scáth thír.

Sin mo scéal.

Crazyhorse's Last Dream

I

Here's a story for you –

Sacred trees
whose arms touched the skies,
hacked down and turned into
thousands of tiny houses.

Bright, beautiful rivers
dark red now
with the innards of the Black Mountains.

Wide prairies, deep glens
cut up into thousands
of garden strips.

Birds of the air
gone over seas,
the eagle's eggs
smashed to pieces.

The wolf silent
under a cold, blood red moon.

Backs of wild horses
buckled under the saddle
of a fat christian.

Soft, bountiful breasts
covered up for the shame-
faced philosophy of a preacher.

My people's ancient gods
buried alive by the new religion
of a priest.

My friends' unbending shoulders
hidden by the blue coats
of an army.

Fierce, proud warriors
who fought bravely at my side
now puppets to whiskey.

Bones poking out
through the face
of a starving child

as thousands of buffalo
rot in the hot air
of the empty prairie.

II

And what would I, Crazyhorse,
do – if I was to live?
Where would I go in this desert?
Where would I find rest?

Where would I hear a singer
chanting songs of the ancient battles?

Aren't they silenced
by the screaming guns?

And where would I hear
the drums beating?

Aren't they drowned out
by the dull thud
of marching feet?

And where would I hear
the soft, sweet tongues
of the Sioux, the Cheyenne, the Apache?

Don't they speak now with the tongue
of a stranger?

Everything is gone,
the world is closing.
It's only a dream,
a shadowland.

– There's my story.

(trans. by Frank Sewell)

COLETTE NÍ GHALLCHÓIR

Colette was born in the Donegal Gaeltacht in the early 1950s. At the age of ten, she and her family moved to Gaoth Dobhair. Later, while studying in Dublin to become a teacher, she read contemporary poetry. In 1990-91, she earned a place in the Nation-wide Writers' Workshop, supervised by Alan Titley. Since then, she has had poems published in many journals in Ireland and abroad, including Poetry Ireland and Force Ten. In 1996, Colette was nominated for the Pushkin Educators Award for teaching children to write poetry. She currently teaches in Letterkenny, and she has published one collection of poems, 'Idir Dhá Ghleann' (Dublin: Coiscéim, 1999).

Dealán an Aoibhnis

Nuair a las mé an dealán
fadó ar an teallach,
rith mé leis ar fud an tí
go háthasach.
Bagraíodh orm,
ach dúirt mo sheanathair leo -
'Lig di, lig di,
níl gar a bheith léi,
lasfaidh sise i gcónaí
na dealáin is mian léi.'

Sparkler

When I lit the sparkler
years ago on the hearth,
I ran around the house with it,
in sheer delight.
I was told off
but my granda told them:
'Let her be. Let her be.
You're wasting your breath.
She'll always light up
whatever sparkler she wants.'

(trans. by Frank Sewell)

Billy Wright

Tá an laoch ar lár,
caillte.
Ná caoinígí é,
ní bheadh sé ag súil leis.
Saighdiúir a bhí ann.
'Sé an bás a ba dhual dó.
Ní raibh sé ag súil
a bheith i ndeireadh
na péice ar leaba
a bhí leagtha
le síoda bán.
Ní bhfuair sé
ach an bás cruaidh sin
a dháil sé,
go minic,
ar a naimhde.

Billy Wright

The warrior is dead,
finished.
Do not mourn him.
He wouldn't have expected it.
He was a soldier,
and death was natural to him.
He never expected
to breathe his last
on a well-made bed
with a silk white sheet.
He simply came
to the same cruel end
he so often dealt out
to his enemy.

(trans. by Frank Sewell)

Buíochas

Íosfaidh mé na grabhrógaí
a thiteann ó thábla an mháistir.
Ní scaipeann sé mórán acu,
ach corruair bíonn sé ag amharc orm,
deireann sé:
'Tá ocras uirthise.'
Leis sin,
scuabann sé a mhéar bheag ar an línéadach gheal,
agus síos leo.
Liomsa iad,
ach bím ag amharc
ar an bhéile bhreá aigesean.

Thanks a Lot

I will eat the crumbs
that fall from the master's table.
He doesn't share them much
but the odd time he looks at me
and says:
'She is hungry.'
With that,
he rubs his little finger on the white tablecloth, and
hands them
down to me;
but I keep looking
at the full meal he gets.

(trans. by Frank Sewell)

Éalú

An dtig linn an baile seo a fhágáil
go dtí go dtiteann cuirtíní beaga na gcomharsan?
An dtig linn éalú ó shúile
coimhéadach na gcoinín sin
atá ag léimnigh tríd portach
seo na teorann?
An dtig linn slán a fhágáil
ag lucht na cúlchainte
atá ag brú bás ar ár ngrá,
nó an gcuirfidh muid
an grá seo
amuigh udaí ag áit an tSeantí,
faoi scraithe an bhróin,
faoi chréafóg seo an fhuatha,
í a chur síos
sa dóigh go bhfásfaidh
blátha bána an earraigh
aníos uirthi?
Luífidh sí ansin go suaimhneach
ar feadh na gcianta,
go dtí go bhfásfaidh sé arís,
lá éigin,
mar a d'fhás sé cheana,
gan fhios,
gan choinne,
gan iaraidh,
gan fháilte agus gan bhláth.

Escape

Can we just leave this town,
and let the curtains stop twitching?
Can we escape the watchful eyes
of those rabbits skipping over
the boggy border?
Can we say goodbye
to the backbiters
who want our love put down,
or will we bury this love
somewhere out there
in the earth near Seantí,
in sorrow and in hate,
bury it
until white spring flowers
will grow up out of it?
It'll rest in peace there
for ages,
until it grows again,
one day,
as it did before,
unrecognised
and unexpected,
without invitation
or welcome,
and without coming
to fruition.

(trans. by Frank Sewell)

I nGairdín na n-Úll

Dá mbeinn óg arís,
is tusa óg arís,
i ngairdín na n-úll,

do bhronnfainn ort
an t-úll ba dheirge
ar an gcrann

go bhfeicfinn
an solas,
mar lasair thintrí i do shúile.

Bheadh fuaim
na toirní
amuigh udaí
idir na hEachlaí

's muidne,
ar ár suaimhneas
ag dáileadh na dtorthaí
b'aibí ar a chéile,
ceann ar cheann.

In the Orchard

If I was young again,
and you were young again,
in the orchard,

I would give you
the reddest apple
on the tree

to see the light
burn like flames of fire
in your eyes.

Thunder
would sound
somewhere out there
between the Eachlaí

and us –
happy and content,
sharing out with each other
the ripest fruits,
one after the other.

(trans. by Frank Sewell)

TARLACH MacCONGÁIL

Born in 1976, Tarlach studied Law and French at the Universities of Galway and Poitiers, as well as International Human Rights Law at the University of Essex. Following stints working for a number of international human rights organisations, he is now an editor and researcher at the University of Amsterdam. He has also spent a year teaching English and Irish at the University of Lille. He has won a number of literary competitions, including those at Slógadh and An tOireachtas. His work in the Irish language has been published in several newspapers and journals, most notably, Foinse, but also The Irish Times, Comhar, Innti, An tUltach and Anois; a selection of his poems was published in an anthology entitled 'An Chéad Chló', edited by Cathal Ó Searcaigh (Indreabhán: Cló Iar-Chonnachta, 1997). Tarlach provides his own translations for the poems which follow.

An tUaireadóir

Is deacair glacadh leis go bhfuil m'uaireadóir briste.
Bhí sé lonrach in ainneoin a mhóraoise
agus chomh riachtanach céana agam leis an gcéad lá riamh.
Bronntanas Nollag a bhí ann a fuair mé i mí na gCuach:
mhéadaigh an mhoill mo dhúil ann.
Bhí mé ag síorsmaoineamh ar an uaireadóir uaidh sin amach,
cé go mbíodh sé scaití sa bhaile agus mé ar shiúl,
nó i dteach carad nó in aiteanna eile.

Is deacair glacadh leis nach ndeiseofar m'uaireadóir go brách,
agus nach ndéanfaidh mé fiodrince lucháireach leis arís.
Níl ceannach ar sheoid d'uaireadóir mar é –
taisce mo chuimhní, uaireadóir mo bheatha
ar eagraíodh gach uile rud beo lena chúnamh:
níl athghabháil ar an sonas a bhí.
Tá an todhchaí go léir san aimsir chaite.

The Watch

It is hard to accept that my watch is broken:
It sparkled in defiance of its years
And remained as essential to me as ever before.
A Christmas present received in the Cuckoo month;
My desire for it whetted by the wait;
It filled my thoughts from that day forth,
Even when it would be left at home or
At a friend's or in other places
And me away.

It is hard to accept that my watch is beyond repair,
That it will never again be party to any joyous twirling.
No price can be put on such a gem of a watch:
A trove of memories; the watch of my life
That helped to regulate everything.
There can be no retrieval of happiness past:
The future itself has expired.

Crá an Scoláire

Chrom an sárscoláire
Ar a leabhair agus leis an aois;
íota intleachtúil dá chrá.
Shlog siar bolgam mór léinn,
ach ghargaigh an deoch úd i gcoineascar a shaoil:
a bheatha ar fad caite aige i dtumha a oifige,
b'uaigneach é, gan aige ach
eolas agus tarcaisne
mar chéilí leapa.

The Scholar's Suffering

The great scholar
Is bent over his books and with age.
Tormented by intellectual thirst,
He drank a great draught of learning
That soured in the twilight of a life
Spent in his office-tomb;
Lonely, with only
Knowledge and contempt
As bedfellows.

MARY REID

Mary was born in 1953 in Paite Gabha, Dun na nGall / Donegal, 'ar an teorann idir thuaidh's theas, agus ar imeall Loch Dearg idir neamh agus ifreann!' / on the border between north and south, and by the shores of Loch Derg between heaven and hell. She studied creative writing at Teach na hÉigse / The Poet's House in Donegal, under the tutelage of James Simmons and Cathal Ó Searcaigh, and recently won a prize in the Strokestown Annual Poetry Competition, 2002.

Brocach

Thóg na Gaill
a gcéad ndún in Uladh
in aice le Cúl Raithin:
d'fhógair
Uí Néill é féin
rí ar Éirinn
chuir sé i gcoinne
Cúl Raithin:
níor aithin na Dálaigh
ríocht Uí Néill
chuir siad ina choinne:
loiteadh an Dálach -
leagadh ina chóma é
i lár an chatha,
spreag sé bua
fad is a bhásaigh sé:
cuireadh an Dálach
i nDún na nGall:
an bhliain dár gcionn
crochadh cloigeann
Uí Néill ar spíce
i dtír na nGall:

Badgers' den

The English built
their first fort in Ulster
near Coleraine:
the O'Neill
proclaiming himself
king of the Irish
attacked
Coleraine:
the O'Donnells did not bow
to O'Neill's rule
they attacked him:
the O'Donnell was wounded -
they laid him in his coffin
at the heart of the battle,
he urged them to victory
as he lay dying:
O'Donnell was buried
in Donegal:
the following year
O'Neill's head was displayed
on a spike
in England:

chaoin an file	a poet lamented
na Gaeil	the orphaned
thréigthe	Irish

I

Tochlaíonn an broc	The badger burrows
faoí thalamh	underground
ag tógáil dúnta	building forts
agus cathracha	and cities

bhí fear ag tiomáint	a man was driving
i gceantar sléibhe	in the dark mountains
i dtír na Néilleach	of O'Neill's country

bhuail sé i gcoinne	he hit something
rud inteacht – broc?	– a badger?
bhí eagla air go raibh	he feared he had
ainmhí gonta aige	hurt an animal

ní fhaca sé tada	he saw nothing
gan faic amuigh,	there was nothing out there,
gan le clois	no sound
ach trup an veain	but the whirr
ag tiontú	of the van turning

ag tiontú aríst dó	coming back
scanraigh strainséir é:	a stranger frightened him:
bhí fear ina shuí	a man was sitting
ina shuí ag a thaobh	sitting by his side
ansiúd ar a chlé	there on the left
ar thaobh an phaisinéir	in the passanger seat

'an raibh síob uaidh?'	'did he need a lift?'

ní bhfuair sé freagra	he got no answer
lean siad leo ina dtost	they continued in silence
gan focal astu	without a word out of them
bhí an fear	the man
ag glioscarnaigh	was glistening
é gléasta go h-údárasach	dressed officiously
i gcóta báistí,	in a raincoat,
léim sé amach	he jumped out
in aice le Cúl Raithin.	near Coleraine.

II

Cosnaíonn an broc	The badger guards
brocach go fíochmhar	his den fiercely
le córas míleata	with military orders
lá arna mhárach	the next day
d'fhógar an raidió	the radio announced
gur scaoileadh péas	a peeler had been shot
in aice le Cúl Raithin	near Coleraine
bhí sé 'off duty',	he was 'off duty',
é gléasta go h-údárasach	dressed officiously
ag glioscarnaigh	glistening
i gcóta báistí,	in a rain coat,
nuair a básaíodh é	when he was killed
bhí eagla	the driver
ar an tiománaí	feared
gurb é	that
taibhse an phéas	the ghost of the peeler
a ghlac síob	had taken a lift
ina chuideachta	in his company

dar le	the driver's wife
bean an tiománaí	believed
gurb é	that it was
an fear gunna	the sniper
a ghlac síob	who had taken the lift
ina shuí ag a thaobh	sitting by his side
ansúid ar a chlé	there on his left
ar thaobh an phaisinéir	in the passenger seat

III

III

Iompraíonn broc
suthanna ar feadh míonna
i ndiaidh a nginte

A badger carries
embryoes for months
after conception

an bhliain dár gcionn
bhí fear ag tiomáint
i gceantar sléibhe
i dtír na Néilleach

the following year
a man was driving
in the dark mountains
of O'Neill's country

bhuail sé i gcoinne
rud inteacht – broc?
bhí eagla air go raibh
ainmhí gonta aige

he hit something
– a badger?
he feared he had
hurt an animal

ní fhaca sé tada
gan faic amuigh,
gan le clois
ach trup an veain
ag tiontú

he saw nothing
there was nothing out there,
no sound
but the whirr
of the van turning

gan deifir air
tiontú aríst
ar eagla go mbeadh

he was in no hurry
back
for fear there would be

stráinséir ag a thaobh
ina shuí ar a chlé
ansúid
ar thaobh an phaisinéir

ach b'é broc
a bhí roimhe
ina luí ar a dhroim
gonta go dona

IV

Iompraíonn broic
suthanna go mbíonn
siad réidh lena gcothú

d'éirigh dhá bhroc eile
amach as brocach
thug céim chun tosaigh
trasna an bhóthair
thug siad uillinn

don taismeach
d'ardaigh siad é
go leathanghuailleach,
d'iompar siad leo é
go mall, tórramhach

tá na mílte míle
brocacha
idir dúnta na Néilleach
agus dún na nDálach

a stranger at his side
sitting on his left
there
in the passenger seat

but it was a badger
that lay before him
lying on its back
badly hurt

IV

The badger carries
embryoes until it is ready
to nurture them

two other badgers appeared
from a den
they marched forward
across the road
they shouldered

the injured badger
raising him
across the broad of their back
they carried him away
slowly, in funeral procession

there are thousands of miles
of badgers' dens
between the forts of the O'Neills
and the fort of O'Donnell